Translated Texts for Byzantinists

The intention of the series is to broaden access to Byzantine texts from 800 AD, enabling students, non-specialists and scholars working in related disciplines to access material otherwise unavailable to them. The series will cover a wide range of texts, including historical, theological and literary works, all of which include an English translation of the Byzantine text with introduction and commentary.

Liverpool University Press gratefully acknowledges the generous support of Dr Costas Kaplanis, alumnus of King's College London, who suggested the idea of the series to Professor Herrin and has underwritten the initial expenses.

T0341636

Translated Texts for Byzantinists
Volume 2

A Tale of Two Saints

The Martyrdoms and Miracles of Saints Theodore 'the Recruit' and 'the General'

Critical introduction, translation and commentary by
JOHN HALDON

Liverpool
University
Press

First published 2016
Liverpool University Press
4 Cambridge Street
Liverpool, L69 7ZU

British Library Cataloguing-in-Publication Data
A British Library CIP Record is available.

ISBN 978 1 78138 282 0 cased
ISBN 978 1 78138 166 3 limp

Typeset by Carnegie Book Production, Lancaster
Printed and bound by CPI Group (UK) Ltd, Croydon CR0 4YY

CONTENTS

ILLUSTRATIONS

ACKNOWLEDGEMENTS

As usual, a number of colleagues and friends deserve thanks for their help and advice, most particularly Alice-Mary Talbot, who generously read through the translation and saved me from a number of errors; Meaghan McEvoy, who read through and offered valuable comments and criticism on the whole manuscript; and Claudia Rapp, who reviewed chapters 1 and 2 and made valuable critical comments and constructive suggestions. I owe thanks to those members of my graduate seminar who contributed to the translation of Text 5 (Skyler Anderson, Walter Beers, Lorenzo Bondioli, Megan Garedakis and Vicky Hioureas), and, of course, to the anonymous reviewers for a number of helpful suggestions and corrections. Needless to say, any shortcomings in the volume are my responsibility alone.

ABBREVIATIONS

AB *Analecta Bollandiana*

ACO II, 2. ii *Acta Conciliorum Oecumenicorum* II, 2.1–2: *Concilium universale Constantinopolitanum tertium*, ed. R. Riedinger (Berlin 1990–1992)

AS *Acta Sanctorum* (Antwerp 1643ff.)

B *Byzantion*

BBS *Berliner Byzantinistische Studien*

BCH *Bulletin de Correspondance Hellénique*

BHG F. Halkin, *Bibliotheca Hagiographica Graeca* (Subsidia hagiographica 8a. 3rd edn (Brussels 1957)

BHG, Auct. F. Halkin, *Novum Auctarium Bibliothecae Hagiographicae Graecae* (Subsidia hagiographica 65. Brussels 1959)

BMGS *Byzantine and Modern Greek Studies*

BZ *Byzantinische Zeitschrift*

CCSG *Corpus Christianorum, series Graeca*

CFHB *Corpus Fontium Historiae Byzantinae*

CJ *Corpus Juris Civilis* II: *Codex Iustinianus*, ed. P. Krüger (Berlin, 1892–1895, repr. 1945–1963)

CPG M. Geerard, *Clavis Patrum Graecorum*, I–IV (Turnhout 1983, 1974, 1979, 1980); M. Geerard and F. Glorie, V (Turnhout 1987)

CSHB *Corpus Scriptorum Historiae Byzantinae*

CTh. *Theodosiani libri xvi cum constitutionibus Sirmondianis*, eds Th. Mommsen, P. Meyer et al. (Berlin 1905)

DOP *Dumbarton Oaks Papers*

DOS Nesbitt, J. and N. Oikonomidès, *Catalogue of Byzantine Seals at Dumbarton Oaks and in the Fogg Museum of Art*, I: *Italy, North of the Balkans, North of the Black Sea* (Washington D.C., 1991); II: *South of the Balkans, the Islands, South of Asia Minor* (Washington D.C., 1994); III: *West, Northwest and Central Asia Minor and the Orient* (Washington D.C., 1996); IV: *The East,* ed. E. McGeer, J. Nesbitt and N. Oikonomidès (Washington D.C., 2001); V: *The East (continued), Constantinople and environs, unknown locations, addenda, uncertain readings*, ed. E. McGeer, J. Nesbitt and N. Oikonomidès† (Washington D.C., 2005)

EA   *Epigraphica Anatolica*

EEBS   Ἐπετηρὶς Ἑταιρείας Βυζαντινῶν Σπουδῶν

EO   *Échos d'Orient*

JGR   *Jus Graecoromanum*, eds I. and P. Zepos, 8 vols (Athens, 1931/ Aalen, 1962)

JHS   *Journal of Hellenic Studies*

JöB   *Jahrbuch der österreichischen Byzantinistik*

JRS   *Journal of Roman Studies*

JThS   *Journal of Theological Studies*

KP   Ziegler, K. and W. Sontheimer, eds, *Der kleine Pauly. Lexikon der Antike in fünf Bänden* (Munich 1979)

Not. Dig. See Seeck 1876

NPB   Mai, A. 1852–1854. *Nova Patrum Bibliotheca*, vols i–vii (Rome); Cozza-Luzi, G. 1871–1905, vols viii–x (Rome)

ODB   Kazhdan, A.P. et al., *The Oxford Dictionary of Byzantium* (Oxford–New York 1991)

PG   *Patrologiae Cursus completus*, series Graeco-Latina, ed. J.-P. Migne (Paris 1857–1866, 1880–1903)

PLRE   Jones, A.H.M., J.R. Martindale and J. Morris, *The prosopography of the later Roman Empire* 1. *A.D. 260–395*; 2. *A.D. 395–527*; 3/1–2 *A.D. 527–641* (Cambridge 1971–1992)

PmbZ   Lilie, R.-J., C. Ludwig, T. Pratsch, I. Rochow et al., *Prosopographie der mittelbyzantinischen Zeit. Erste Abteilung (641–867)*, 1–6 (Berlin–New York 1999–2002); *Zweite Abteilung (867–1025)*, 1–8 (Berlin–New York 2013) (numbers of entries are consecutive through both series)

RE   *Paulys Realencyclopädie der classischen Altertums Wissenschaft, neue Bearbeitung*, ed. G. Wissowa, I/1 (Stuttgart 1893) – XXIII/2 (1959) with index of additions; XXIV (1963); I/A1 (1914) – X/A (1972); Suppl. I (1903) – XIV (1974)

REB   *Revue des Études Byzantines*

ROC   *Revue de l'Orient Chrétien*

TU   *Texte und Untersuchungen zur altchristlichen Literatur*

ZV   Zacos, G. and A. Veglery, *Byzantine Lead Seals*, vol. I, parts 1–3 (Basel 1972)

FOREWORD

St Theodore *tērōn* (τήρων, 'the Recruit') numbered among the most popular saints of the Byzantine world from the later fourth century, and is attributed with working a number of miracles through his intercession with God on behalf of those who prayed to him or visited his churches, especially that at Euchaïta. This small provincial settlement had, by the later fourth century, as Gregory of Nyssa informs us, become a flourishing centre of worship and devotion to him. By the later ninth century a second Theodore, the *stratēlatēs*/στρατηλάτης, or 'the General', had appeared, a product of the particular social and cultural context of the middle of the ninth century and afterwards. At the same time the iconography of the saint was developing apace, with the second Theodore appearing from the tenth century, although the difference between the two in representation is not always clearly made without an accompanying textual indication. The iconography of both saints Theodore has been thoroughly examined in a number of studies, and need not detain us here, except to note that the evolution of the accounts of the martyrdom is paralleled by the evolution of the two versions of the saint in the visual tradition.[1] The present translation of and commentary on two collections of miracles and five martyrdom accounts of the two saints Theodore grew out of work related to the Avkat Archaeological Project, a survey of the area of ancient Euchaïta in north-central Turkey, chiefly because of the topical interest of the second collection, which was probably compiled in the later seventh or perhaps the early eighth century. This short collection (*BHG* 1764) is of primary importance for the history of the Byzantine world in the seventh century not only for the detail it offers about life in a provincial town during a period of warfare and invasion but also because it is the only account of any kind – hagiographical or other – from this period written from a local perspective about a provincial city, apart from the much better-known and better-studied miracles of St Demetrius in Thessaloniki: all our other sources, with very few exceptions at this time,

---

1 See Walter 1999; 2003a; 2003b.

are written from a Constantinopolitan perspective. The miracles tell us about the physical appearance of the city, about the reaction of its populace to attack and the devastation wrought by the invaders, and about the role of the cult of St Theodore and the nature of popular piety in the provinces. It presents, in short, a graphic illustration of life for some of the inhabitants of a seventh-century Byzantine province.

Scholars of hagiography (Delehaye, Halkin), of the history of Byzantine art (Walter) and of early Byzantium (Kazhdan, Trombley, Zuckerman, Artun) have all devoted studies to various aspects of the cult of St Theodore or to the miracles, especially to those in *BHG* 1764, and what follows owes a great deal to their work. In the discussion of the texts, below, I will argue that the text of *BHG* 1764 is undoubtedly a product of the last years of the tenth or more probably the middle years of the eleventh century, but that we can detect a number of layers, the earliest of which is equally clearly to be located in the later seventh century. All the texts presented here merit further discussion, because a careful examination reveals a good deal about both the stages of evolution through which these accounts went and the process of incremental change that produced the versions that are extant today. In addition, and as intimated above, the results of recent archaeological research in the region of Euchaïta can now be brought into the picture to throw new light on some of the written evidence.

The relationship of the texts to one another and their likely dates of composition will be considered in detail in Chapter 2. The earliest collection (*BHG* 1765c) has remained for the most part neglected except for the publications of its first editor, Sigalas, in the 1920s and 1930s, although Delehaye devoted some attention to it. Unlike the later martyrdom account and the miracles found in *BHG* 1764, it represents a very different, perhaps more traditional, collection, written down in the second half of the fifth century and characteristic of much similar late antique hagiographical writing. Roughly contemporary with the better-known collection of the miracles of St Thekla, it merits greater attention not only for its historical and cultural–historical value but also because it offers a useful comparison and contrast with the later collection. While some of the miracle stories circulated independently, they were generally transmitted – and heard – in the context of accounts of the passion or martyrdom of the saint and, in order to retain the context within which these collections were presented and used, I have therefore also included some versions of these accounts, since they also cast important light on the date of composition and the evolution of such collections.

Miracle stories and martyrdom accounts were a fundamental element in Byzantine and medieval Christian culture in general: they were a means of representing the relationship between the human and the divine, the secular and the sacred; and of confirming the perceptions of the listener that they belonged to a community of the faithful united by a common history of struggle against evil and that there were inspiring models to follow in dealing with adversity, both personal and communal. In what follows we will look at the content of the miracle collections, with their highly local relevance, as well as at the ways in which both miracle stories and martyrdom accounts reflected changing social and economic relationships across several centuries. Both miracle stories and accounts of the martyrdom offer information to the modern reader about day-to-day life, the assumptions and beliefs of the 'ordinary' recipient of the stories and the form and content of particular saints' cults. In presenting for the first time a translation of these particular texts into English, I hope I have made more accessible to non-specialists in particular some key documents from the cultural world of the eastern Roman empire, documents that reveal some aspects of what Norman Baynes called 'the thought-world of east Rome'.

1 The two Saints Theodore: the Harbaville triptych
(Louvre, tenth century, ivory)

INTRODUCTION

St Theodore 'the Recruit'

St Theodore 'the Recruit' (*tērōn*), martyred at Amasia under Maximian (Galerius) and Maximinus (Daia), was one of the best known and most popular of the Byzantine warrior-saints, perhaps at least as popular as St George or St Demetrius and probably more so than St Merkourios, St Procopius or St Eutropios, among others.[1] He is associated in his *Passio* with the city of Amasia and the nearby settlement or estate of Euchaïta. The latter is not known before the Roman period, and remained until the later fourth century a small rural settlement or estate within the territory of the city of Amasia.[2] Although his remains were quite soon after his death transferred to Euchaïta, Amasia was apparently the original place of both the martyrdom and the burial of Theodore, and remained a focus for devotion – indeed, in the final lines of one, probably later, account of the martyrdom reference is made to a disagreement between the people of Amasia and those of Euchaïta about where his remains should be interred.[3] John Mauropous, the eleventh-century metropolitan of Euchaïta, mentions a wondrous column to which the saint had been bound during his torture, still to be seen in his day in the city; and a much earlier inscription of the emperor Anastasius (491–518) now in Amasia probably refers to Euchaïta, when it mentions Theodore as the guardian of 'this city'.[4]

Euchaïta owed its importance almost entirely to the fact that the remains of St Theodore were buried there. A flourishing focus for

---

1 See Beck 1959: 405; Delehaye 1909, 2–4; Walter 1999; 2003b.

2 Described in the metaphrastic passio of Theodore (*BHG* 1763, ed. Delehaye 1909: 146.22) as ἐν χωρίῳ Εὐχάϊτα λεγομένῳ ... ὑπὸ τὴν τῶν Ἀμασέων μητρόπολιν. For the history and archaeology of Euchaïta, see Haldon et al. 2007, 2009 and 2010; for Amasia: Beck 1959: 166–167.

3 André 1891; Sigalas 1937: 84, and discussion of the texts, below.

4 De Lagarde 1882: 130–137 (*BHG* 1771); Delehaye 1925a: 24; Mango and Ševčenko 1972: 382–384.

honouring the saint, it attracted visitors and pilgrims as early as the later fourth century AD and, along with several other sites, grew into one of the foremost pilgrimage centres in Anatolia.[5] A panegyric composed in the late fourth or very early fifth century devoted to the saint, and attributed to Gregory of Nyssa (*BHG* 1760), represents possibly the earliest version of the martyrdom, upon which all subsequent more elaborate versions were based. According to the legend, which in its basic outlines seems to have been well established by the end of the fourth century, the body of St Theodore was taken from Amasia and interred at Euchaïta. Reference to the pious Eusebia, who performed this act of devotion, appears already in the encomium by Chrysippos, written in the 450s or 460s (see below).[6] The pious woman who takes and preserves the martyr's remains was, of course, a common motif in many ancient martyrologies, as the pun on the name itself suggests.[7] While the translation of a saint's remains becomes a usual feature of martyrdom accounts and hagiographies, this is a relatively early occurrence. The first recorded transfer is that of the remains of St Babylas in the early 350s by the Caesar Constantius Gallus, from the saint's original burial place near Antioch to the specially built church in the suburb of Daphne. The event was described a little later in a homily of John Chrysostom.[8] When exactly the translation of Theodore's remains actually took place remains unclear, but the church of Theodore at Euchaïta soon became the centre of a busy pilgrim traffic – according to Gregory of Nyssa, 'we celebrate this day with annual feasts and yet the stream of people arriving here because of their zeal for the martyrs never ceases', and Gregory's *ekphrasis* of the church has justly been seen as a masterpiece of the genre.[9] Chrysippos of Jerusalem likewise points to the flow of pilgrims from far and wide, a sentiment (and, of course, a topos) repeated in later accounts of the martyrdom as well as by John Mauropous.[10]

---

5 See Limberis 2011: 20; Hellenkemper 1995; Vryonis 1981.

6 By the middle Byzantine period Eusebia herself had also become the object of public devotion and veneration: Delehaye 1909: 40–41; 192. 13–22, 193. 3–11.

7 Delehaye 1909: 40.

8 Babylas had been bishop of Antioch during the persecution of Decius, under whom he died in 253. See *BHG* 205–206 (*Passio*); for John Chrysostom see Schatkin et al. 2004 (*BHG* 207).

9 Ed. Cavarnos, 70. 1f.; trans. Leemans, 90. Detailed discussion: Limberis 2011: 55–62.

10 See Sigalas 1937: 84–85; and 58.11–15; Delehaye 1909: 193. 28–30; de Lagarde 1882: 130–137 (*BHG* 1771), esp. 132.

Scholars such as Delehaye and Walter have emphasised the fact that the influence of the cult seems to have expanded quite rapidly from the fourth century – churches and chapels dedicated to the saint were to be found in such widely different places as Constantinople (where later the saint exercised a particular protection over the city and where the patrician Sphorakios built a church in the saint's honour in the 450s),[11] Edessa, Gerasa, Jerusalem, Rome, north Africa and probably the Balkans.[12] Images of St Theodore appear from as early as the fifth and sixth centuries.[13] In the first half of the sixth century the western pilgrim Theodosius mentions the *Civitas Euchaïta, ubi est sanctus martyr Theodorus*,[14] that had by then become an important centre of pilgrimage: the Patriarch Eutychius (552–565) halted at Euchaïta on his way through as he was returning from Amasia to Constantinople[15] and Alypius the stylite visited in the early seventh century.[16] At the same period the monk John the Anchorite visited Euchaïta and the church of St Theodore, possibly on a number of occasions, as he was wont to travel from cult centre to cult centre,[17] and in the tenth century it was known that the shield of St Theodore was hung in the church dedicated to the saint at Dalisandos in Isauria.[18]

The origins of the cult of St Theodore must be understood in the context of the development of the veneration of 'soldier saints' more generally. And although this is not the place to review the extensive literature on the subject, the beginnings of Theodore's cult are reasonably well understood – at least as well understood as the evidence permits, as a number of recent studies have made clear.[19] Theodore seems already by the sixth century,

11 On the rapid spread of St Theodore's cult: Delehaye 1925a: 23–26; Walter 1999: 170–172; Grotowski 2010: 101–102. For the churches see Janin 1969: 148–154, and on Sphorakios' church 152–153; Walter 2003b: 49–50. For Sp(h)orakios see *PLRE* 2: 1026–1027 (Fl. Sporacius 3).

12 Delehaye 1909: 13–14. For the wider tradition, outside the medieval east Roman world, see Moralee 2006; Winstedt 1910; Zandee 1983; and for N. Africa, see Conant 2012: 343. For the Balkans, see the discussion in Walter 2003b: 52–53; for Edessa, Segal 1970: 88; Jerash/Gerasa, Crowfoot 1929; for Jerusalem Maraval 1985: 268.

13 Grotowski 2010: 60–61, n. 13; Walter 2003b: 55–56.

14 See for Theodosius: *Itinera Hierosolymitana*, 144.

15 *Vita Eutychii*, 2355C.

16 *Vita Alypii Stylita*, 152. 11–13.

17 *PG* 87C, 3052B (cap. 180; trans. Wortley, p. 150). On the spread of Theodore's cult: Walter 2003b: 49–50.

18 *De Them.*, 77. 20–21, see also Delehaye 1925a: 24–25.

19 See, in particular, and for a careful and detailed analysis of the cults of Theodore, George and Demetrios in particular, White 2013: 13–93; also Walter 2003a; 2003b; 1999.

certainly by the later seventh, to have been associated with the slaying of a dragon, as seals of the bishops of Euchaita dated to the later sixth, seventh and eighth centuries showing the figure of the saint impaling a dragon illustrate. In this he was not alone, although the dragon motif underwent several changes across the period from the sixth or seventh century into the tenth and eleventh centuries and beyond.[20] Representations of Theodore and the dragon were by the tenth century to be found as far afield as on the church of the holy cross at Aght'amar in Armenia as well as in other Caucasian contexts of the ninth–tenth centuries, in rock-cut churches in Cappadocia, or on an icon in the monastery of St Catherine on Mt Sinai.[21] According to the developed version of the legend, the saint killed the fearsome serpent near Euchaïta, a point which increased his popularity considerably and seems to have contributed to a further expansion of the repertoire of both stories and miracles. Like many saint's cults in Anatolia, as well as elsewhere, Theodore's was probably bound up, if not directly then by context and local tradition, with earlier non-Christian beliefs, heroes and practices, and there is probably some connection between the cult of Theodore and ancient Anatolian traditions of the Holy Rider. And the dragon was, of course, symbolic of evil and of Satan.[22] In Chrysippos' encomium Theodore is credited with ridding the district around Euchaïta of an infestation of serpents and other beasts, and it has been suggested that this early account may thus be a first, dim reflection of the origins of the presence of the cult at Euchaïta.[23] Whether this act can be connected with the suggestion that Theodore's cult at Euchaïta was imposed upon an earlier pagan cult – perhaps that of the central Anatolian deity Mēn (who is also found represented on occasion mounted, with a lance, trampling an ox-head) and/or that of the Holy Rider – remains unclear.[24] It is worth

20 Grotowski 2010: 79, 92–94; White 2008 for further treatment of the dragon motif.

21 For Aght'amar: Der Nersessian 1965: 18–20, fig. 50; for Cappadocia and Georgia: Thierry 1999 and 1972 (although with a doubtful seventh-century suggested date for the Cappadocian church); and for St Catherine: Weitzmann 1976: 71–73 and pl. B33–34. See in general on the imagery of St Theodore Walter 2003a.

22 For examples and discussion see Trombley 1993–1994; Arnold 1995; for Theodore: Pancaroğlu 2004: esp. 151–156. The dragon symbolising evil: Chapter 3, n. 21 below.

23 Although Hengstenberg 1912/1913: 95 argued that the two stories were quite distinct and developed independently. In either case, the snake was a symbol of evil and in representational terms was frequently employed to indicate a persecutor, and this allusion was doubtless not lost on Chrysippos and his audience: see Walter 1999: 178; White 2008: 162–163.

24 See the discussion in Sigalas 1937: 83–85; Lübeck 1910. For Mēn see Lane 1976: 67–80;

noting that in a Coptic fragment of the seventh-century *Life* of the patriarch Benjamin of Alexandria the inhabitants of what appears to be Euchaïta are mentioned in passing as known for their sacrificing to a nearby serpent, perhaps a reflection of an ancient local cult (or a misunderstanding of the Theodore story).[25] But that Theodore replaced an ancient cultic tradition involving a serpent and snakes is not implausible, given the way in which other Christian cults replaced earlier pagan traditions in Asia Minor at this period.[26] Delehaye was extremely dismissive, if not cynical, about tracing any saint's cult back to a pre-Christian context in this way, although more recent scholarship has been somewhat more tolerant in this respect. But, as Delehaye pointed out, the dragon or serpent is an almost universal folk motif, and there is no evidence other than these somewhat allusive references to any such tradition at Amasia or Euchaïta. The question deserves more attention than can be given here, but the work of Pancaroğlu may suggest some possible directions for further research.[27] In any case, the dragon story was certainly in circulation in the Byzantine world by the later seventh century,[28] was known in Egypt already by the same time, and may well have been known in the Balkans already by the fifth century. The story of Theodore and the dragon appears to pre-date that of George and the dragon by some centuries, at least in the iconographic tradition.[29]

Mitchell 1993: 24–25 with references; *KP* 3, 1194–1196; for the Holy Rider see Pancaroğlu 2004: esp. 151–156.

25 Amélineau 1888: 374, and see 'Bulletin des publications hagiographiques', *AB* 29 (1910), 157–239, at 161.

26 See Trombley 1993–1994: 149, 153–56, 159; and cf. Niewöhner et al. 2013: 106–110. The proposal was first argued in detail by Sigalas 1937: 83–84.

27 Pancaroğlu 2004; Delehaye 1909: 113–117.

28 For the beginnings and background of Theodore's dragon-slaying see esp. Walter 2003a; more generally, the careful analysis in White 2008.

29 See Delehaye 1925a: 46–49 for one version of this tale (*BHG* 1766); Walter 2003a; and Walter 2003b: 52–53. The dragon motif itself is ancient, and already in the fifth century appears in episcopal hagiography: see Rapp 2005: 299–300, for example. At some time after the middle of the eighth century the emperor Constantine V was also credited with the slaying of a dragon: see Rochow 1994: 127–128. For George and the dragon: Walter 2003b: 141; Aufhauser 1911.

St Theodore 'the General'

Theodore 'the Recruit' had some regional competition, for by the later ninth century two saints Theodore were venerated: the original, and St Theodore 'the General' (*stratēlatēs*).[30] Theodore the General first appears at this time in literary sources, so his local tradition probably pre-dates this by some years. He was especially popular thereafter among the Anatolian military élite, although in many respects – apart from his promotion to general – the second Theodore is much like the first, and accounts of his martyrdom and early life follow more or less closely the details of those of Theodore the Recruit. The origins of the cult remain unknown: Oikonomidès hypothesised that it reflected the post-iconoclastic misidentification of older images of St Theodore in civilian and in military dress, with the latter being taken as a different saint from the former; in contrast, Walter suggested that it lies in the existence of an earlier and largely forgotten cult of a Theodore who was martyred under Diocletian and was rewarded with the title *stratēlatēs* for his suffering.[31] Hypothetical though they are, neither of these is implausible.

But perhaps more significant is the fact that this change in status was not limited to Theodore alone, since an increasing emphasis on their military status and achievements affected several other 'military' martyrs at this time, including Demetrius, George and Procopius, just as some hagiographies were similarly rewritten to upgrade their heroes – St Ioannikios, for example, transformed in a tenth-century rewriting of his *Life* from a deserter, in the original account, to an officer and commander.[32] While it is surely correct that this reflects an imperial interest, most evident in the writing of Leo VI,[33] we should also take into account the growing

30 See White 2013: 72–74; Grotowski 2010: 118–120, with 101 and n. 147; older literature: Oikonomidès 1986; Walter 1999: 183–189; 2003b: 55–56, 59–66; with Halkin 1963, 1981; and Todt 1996.

31 Grotowski 2010: 117–120; Walter 2003b: 60–61; Oikonomidès 1986: 334–335. See also Weigert 1990.

32 Mango 1983. Background: Sullivan 1998; cf. Efthymiadis 1998: 42–43.

33 See esp. White 2013: 65–93 on the investment by the Macedonian court from the time of Leo VI onwards in the 'corps' of military patrons; and more broadly Riedel 2010. The integration of military and religious agendas with that of the imperial court is an obvious feature from the time of Leo VI, evident in his *Taktika* as well as in other contexts: see Haldon 2014: 15–38. The emperor Basil II is reported to have made a pilgrimage to the tombs of both Theodores, for example, and Isaac Komnenos, brother of the emperor Alexios I, had St Theodore on his seal: Crostini 1996: 78; Holmes 2005: 56 and 218–219.

importance and in particular the increasing self-awareness of the militarised middle Byzantine provincial élite from the middle and later ninth century, especially in the context of the growth of a saint's cult in which the hero is a general of noble birth and high rank, of impeccable moral and religious standing, whose behaviour might serve as a model for the whole social élite.[34] At Dolichē (Dülük) in Commagene a stone slab, probably of the tenth century, with a large sculptured cross and an invocation in Greek to Theodore *stratēlatēs*, stood at a site (Dülük Baba Tepesi) that by the fourteenth century had become an Islamic cult centre. The inscription may illustrate the close association between military elite and St Theodore 'the General': the region was reconquered by East Roman forces under Nicephorus Phocas in 962 and Dolichē itself became the headquarters of the new small *thema* or military district of Teloukh.

It was not simply in respect of their role as heroic fighters for the faith or a reflection of élite values that the military saints occupied such a central place in medieval eastern Roman perceptions. The military saints were also the symbolic bearers of victory over external foes, both real and spiritual. This may also have contributed to the increasingly heroic quality of, as well as the amount of detail given in, accounts of saints' encounters with dragons, a motif that parallels chronologically the rise – or perhaps the reappearance of – aristocratic notions of family honour and genealogy within the east Roman social élite from the later ninth century onwards.[35]

It is important to underline the point that the accounts of Theodore General's life and martyrdom include elements that would be expected in a ninth- or tenth-century version of the deeds of a senior military person: his noble family origins, his easy communication – as a member of the state élite – with the ruler, his integrity and sense of honour. These are all attributes that we find in other sources reflecting élite values and views, and not far removed from those that would have been found also in the originally orally transmitted epic tales of the hero Digenis Akritas, for

---

34 And with the rise to power of the Komnenos family, of course, aristocratic and imperial values merged. On the evolution, values and mores of the middle Byzantine provincial élite from the ninth century onwards see Magdalino 1989; Cheynet 2006b, and other essays in Cheynet 2006a; Haldon 2009; and for the ways in which St Theodore (as well as other martial saints) was deployed on the lead seals of members of the military élite, Cheynet 2003. For hagiographical reflections of social status and related concerns see Patlagean 1981; and for nobility of birth as an attribute of saints Caseau 2009: 140–143. For the inscription see Facella and Stanke 2011: 157–167.

35 See Campagnolo and Weber 2015: 21–23; on the dragon White 2008 with further sources and literature.

example: tales that appear to have come into being at some point during the ninth or tenth century. Indeed, in the metaphrastic *passio* of St Theodore the General the saint's behaviour towards the emperor is not dissimilar to that exhibited by the akritic hero towards the Byzantine emperor during his visit to the provinces.[36] Furthermore, such doubles were not unique – St Sabas the Goth was paired by St Sabas the *stratēlatēs* (although his martyrdom was very different from that of the original Sabas). He also appears in the manuscript tradition for the first time in the ninth century, and probably for the same or very similar reasons as St Theodore the *stratēlatēs*. Likewise, St Andrew the soldier gains a companion, Andrew the *stratēlatēs*.[37] Indicative of the change is the fact that Theodore the Recruit now also appears with many of the attributes of his élite counterpart from the tenth century onwards,[38] and it is not without significance that at the end of the tenth century the general Nikephoros Ouranos, a member of this élite, one of Basil II's most effective commanders and author of a military treatise which incorporated both late Roman and more recent practical military handbooks, composed his own *encomium* of the Recruit, based on the earlier tradition but showing some very marked signs of the influence of the martydrom stories of the General.[39]

The earliest encomium for this general Theodore is that penned by Niketas David of Paphlagonia in the early tenth century;[40] shortly thereafter another eulogy was composed by a certain Euthymios *prōtasēkrētēs/* πρωτασηκρήτης.[41] And, while these writers kept the two Theodores separate, there was clearly some merging of the two; indeed, in some cases churches were dedicated to 'the two Theodores', and they were generally associated from this time in the hagiological and encomiastic literature. John Mauropous, who wrote an epigram on two images of the saint(s), appears to ignore or implicitly deny their separate identities.[42] Certainly

36 See Text 5: §7 and note; and cf. *Digenis*: IV. 971–1053; Trapp 1971: G.IV. 1922–2004; discussion in Jeffreys 2014: 142–144, with earlier literature.

37 Detailed discussion in Follieri 1962; see also Kazhdan 1993.

38 See two versions of the life and martyrdom of Theodore *stratēlatēs* as edited by Delehaye 1909: 151–167, 168–182 (*BHG* 1751 and 1752); and discussion of the texts, below.

39 *BHG* 1762m. See Halkin 1962; cf. also Halkin 1981; Kazhdan 1983: 544–545; Beck 1959: 570 (although not claiming that this was Nikephoros Ouranos).

40 *BHG* 1753, ed. Delehaye 1925a: 83–89, with 13–14 on the mss; on his life and works: *PmbZ* #25712, with Paschalides 1999.

41 *BHG* 1753b, ed. Halkin 1981; see Markopoulos 1986; *PmbZ* #21930.

42 See Delehaye 1909: 15–16 and 35–37; Oikonomidès 1986. For John Mauropous' text: ed. de Lagarde 1882: 36.

by the ninth century the two Theodores were the subject of popular tales as well as liturgical celebration, as the hymns or *kanones* in their honour attributed to an otherwise unknown but probably later ninth-century hymnographer George illustrate.[43] Leo the Deacon reports that the emperor John I Tzimiskes invoked St Theodore the *stratēlatēs* in his battles, and that the mysterious figure seen on a white charger at the battle of Dorostolon in 971 was the saint, come to help the emperor.[44] A good indication of the importance and symbolic value of Theodore the General for the eastern Roman military élite is the fact that by the twelfth century at the latest the epic of Digenis Akritas has the eponymous hero construct a church in honour of Theodore the General within the courtyard of his palace on the Euphrates, in which he inters his father.[45]

In Anatolia Theodore *stratēlatēs* is associated in the sources with another city not far from Euchaïta, named as Euchaïna/Euchaneia (or even Euchaia), where Tzimiskes is reported to have reconstructed the church of St Theodore, changing the name of the town to Theodoroupolis in commemoration of the saint's miraculous support for the imperial forces at the battle of Dorostolon in 971.[46] While some confusion about both Euchaïta–Euchaïna and the two Theodores has reigned among modern historians as well as among contemporaries (already in the eulogy of Euthymios *prōtasēkrētēs* the General is interred at Euchaïta, not Euchaïna),[47] there seems no doubt that the two places were distinct, as convincingly argued by Oikonomidès, and while Leo the deacon, for example, reports that it was Dorostolon/Dristra that the emperor renamed following his victory over the Rus', the later tradition is fairly clear that it was Euchaïna. It is quite possible that John I, who clearly had a particular devotion to the saint, renamed more than one city after him, or named one city after Theodore the Recruit and others, or another,

---

43 Beck 1959: 519; see also 589 for a *kanon* of Athanasius of Athos on the saint; and 698–699 for a miracle collection of Theodore the Recruit by Constantine Akropolites (ca. 1300). Other late works dedicated to one or both Theodores: Beck 1959: 700, 720, 725, 798. Complete list: *BHG* 1760–1773.

44 Leo diac., *Hist.*, ix, 9 [197 and n. 47 Talbot–Sullivan]).

45 *Digenis*: VII. 104–105; Trapp 1971: G. VII. 3240–3246. In general on the akritic epic: Jeffreys 2014: 142–150; Beck 1971: 63–97; for élite values in this period: Magdalino 1989.

46 Zonaras, xvii, 3; Cedrenus, ii, 411. 21. See Leo diac., *Hist.*, ix, 12 (trans. Talbot–Sullivan 200 and n. 67) with brief discussion in Grotowski 2010: 100–102; Oikonomidès 1986: 330 n. 10; and Hutter 1988; Walter 2003b: 56–58. Note also Holmes 2005: 218, n. 113.

47 Van Hooff 1883: 367. 17–19.

after Theodore the General (and there was, in any case, another fortress in the Balkans named Theodoroupolis, mentioned in the sixth century by Procopius).[48]

In respect of the Anatolian city Walter objected that 'two different episcopal sees could hardly have been situated' close to one another, but the evidence seems to suggest otherwise – given the possibility of the church restructuring the local ecclesiastical administrative arrangements (as was done for Euchaïta in the later ninth century, for example), there is no reason why they could not have been. Indeed, according to the *Synaxarion* of Constantinople, Euchaneia is noted explicitly to have been close to Euchaïta.[49] The bishops of Euchaïna/Euchaneia (attested first in the eleventh century) appear in synodal lists along with the bishops of Euchaïta (attested from the early sixth century: see below), and there is an eleventh-century seal of a bishop John of Euchaneia. Lazaros of Galesion in the eleventh century visited Euchaneia and then Euchaïta on his pilgrimage, finding the local inhabitants most unfriendly and being chased by a large black dog! At a Constantinopolitan synod held in 1173 both Constantine of Euchaïta and Leo of Euchaneia were present.[50] The identity and location of Euchaïna remain problematic. Oikonomidès, following references in the thirteenth-century Danişmendname, suggested Çorum, not far to the south-west of Euchaïta, and this seems a likely identification. But it may equally be identified with the nearby village of Çavgan (later Çağna), now Elmapınar, lying a little to the west of Beyözü/ Avkat, where survey work suggests there was once also a church (although the date has not been established).[51]

48 See Proc., *Buildings*, iv, 6 (and cf. iv, 11 for two forts 'of St Theodore'); *RE* V A, 2 (1934): 1920–1921.

49 *Synax. CP*, 35. 33. See Delehaye 1911: 366 on the assumed distance between the two, followed by Oikonomidès 1986: 333; and Walter 2003b: 58.

50 Grégoire, in Anderson et al. 1910: 202–204; Oikonomidès 1986: 332–333, n. 17; *Vita Lazari Gales*, cap. 29 (see Greenfield 2000: 113 and note). For the synodal lists see Darrouzès 1981: 87 (a. 1042); and for the seal: *ZV* I, no. 519; Oikonomidès 1986: 328. This John of Euchaneia may be identified with the bishop of the same name who attended the trial of John Italos in 1082: Grumel–Darrouzès 1989: no. 926. For the synod of 1173: Grumel–Darrouzès 1989: no. 1126.

51 For Çavgan, see TT 387 (1530), under Amasya, p. 388. On Turkish maps of the pre-1960s, the name appears as Çağna. Oikonomidès' argument (1986: 332) was based on the reference in the Danişmendname to the fortress of Yankoniya (or Inigoniya or Nikoniya; the reading is problematic) that was taken by Melik Danişmend after a bitter struggle and was later destroyed in an earthquake, and upon the site of which the Selçuks founded the town of Çorum.

There were several feast-days in honour of St Theodore *tērōn*: the oldest – on 17 February – appears to have been the original date of Theodore's martyrdom; by the eleventh century there were feast-days on the first Saturday of Lent and on 8 June, referred to as the *anthismos/ ἀνθισμός* or *rhodismos/ῥοδισμός*; and a further feast was held on the Saturday of mid-pentecost.[52] This was a special feast for an icon which represented the saint as a *pezos* (foot soldier). The image, depicting him in his military equipment, was supposedly painted at the request of Theodore's patroness Eusebia.[53] One of these feast-days was accompanied by a *panēgyris*, or fair, which attracted pilgrims and merchants and brought considerable wealth into the city.[54] Such fairs were associated across the Byzantine world with saints' feasts and were often major events attracting people from far and wide, including merchants and traders. John Mauropous' writings suggest that the feasts for St Theodore were regularly observed.[55]

There had probably been some confusion about which Theodore was to be celebrated on which feast-day, because in March 1166 the emperor Manuel issued a *novella* stipulating that, among other details, the feast for Theodore *tērōn* was to be observed on 17 February, while those for Theodore the *stratēlatēs* were to be on 7 February, the date of his martyrdom, and 8 June, when the relics were translated from Euchaneia to Serres in Thrace, from where they seem later to have been moved first to Mesembria and then, in 1267, to Venice.[56]

---

52 See Beck 1959: 254–255. For the *anthismos* see the homily of John Mauropous: de Lagarde 1882: 130–137 (*BHG* 1771); and Anrich 1917: 444–449; Peeters 1920: 192–195. In the eastern church the week of mid-Pentecost (Wednesday to Wednesday) occurred midway between Easter and Pentecost. (For the Byzantine liturgical calendar see Beck 1959: 253–262.)

53 For the dates of the feasts, see *Synax. CP*, 451, 469, 735; de Lagarde 1882: no. 179 (119–130), no. 180 (130–137), no. 189 (207–209); Delehaye 1925a: 23–24. The origins of the story about the painting, for which the saint appeared after his death before the painter (who had been commissioned by Eusebia), and its antiquity, are unclear. See Delehaye 1909: 194.9–27; and Delehaye 1966: 276.

54 Delehaye 1925a: 23E f. John Mauropous briefly describes the fair: de Lagarde 1882: no. 180 (131–132). See Vryonis 1981 and Foss 2002.

55 See esp. Vryonis 1981; Limberis 2011.

56 For Manuel's novel, see Macrides 1984: III, 152. 190–191 with commentary at 185. The cult of St Theodore *stratēlatēs* was at Serres by the later twelfth century, as attested by the seal of the metropolitan bishop John, which bears an image of St Theodore together with that of St George (*DOS* I: 42. 4). See Laurent 1963: nos 777 and 778. For the translation to Mesembria and Venice: Delehaye 1925a: 26.

This brings us to a final point, for whereas what purported to be the relics and tomb of Theodore the General were to be seen until the eleventh century, those of Theodore the Recruit were not, or such would appear to have been the case at the time at which John Mauropous was writing. They had previously been dispersed – at least, that is John's explanation for the absence of a tomb, the location of which he apparently does not know. Visitors to Euchaïta came to pray in his church, whereas those who visited Euchaneia came to see the tomb and relics of the General. A later account records that in 1210 the Latin emperor gave the head of St Theodore (presumably the Recruit, since the General's relics, as noted above, had been translated to Serres), along with other relics, to the cardinal Peter, who passed it through his intermediary Clement to the church of the Virgin Mary at Gaeta.[57] From this it seems that some of what were thought to be St Theodore's remains had been in Constantinople, although when they had arrived there remains unclear – perhaps already in the fifth century, when the patrician Sphorakios commissioned the building of his church in honour of the saint. While this remains hypothesis, and the reason for this absence at Euchaïta remains unknown,[58] we may note that in miracle 2 of the eleventh-century collection (dating originally to the seventh century, as we will see), the invading Persians are reported to have ransacked the saint's tomb and taken the remains, which they divided up among themselves. But these were eventually recovered and restored to a resting place in the rebuilt church by the then bishop, Eleutherios (194.30–195.29). In contrast, in miracle 6 the Arabs planned to dig up the church – presumably in search of the tomb and anything of value they might find within it – perhaps suggesting indirectly also that the tomb or at least the relics had been deposited in a location less obvious to an outsider. They were (of course) unsuccessful in their endeavours, because of divine intervention (198.11–15). It is at least possible, therefore, that whatever the reality behind these stories, the dispersal or loss of the relics, or part of them, dates to this period of disruption.

---

57 Source and discussion: Delehaye 1925a: 26.
58 Discussed in Oikonomidès 1986: 328–329.

St Theodore 'the Recruit' and Euchaïta

Theodore the Recruit is firmly associated with the late Roman and Byzantine city of Euchaïta, now identified with the small village of Beyözü, formerly Avkat, some 55 km to the east of Amasia (mod. Amasya) and within the ilçe (sub-province) of Mecitözü, between Amasya and Çorum.[59] Lead seals of the bishops of Euchaïta with the saint and the dragon can be dated in the seventh–eighth centuries, and similar seals depicting the slaying of a dragon have been dated respectively to the years around the middle of the sixth century and the period 650–730.[60] The importance of the cult and of the church in the locality was emphasised by the presence of a version of the apocryphal correspondence between Abgar of Edessa and Christ in an inscription that may have been inserted into the wall of Theodore's church at some point during the fifth century, possibly by a bishop John.[61] Indeed, it was important enough for Euchaïta to have been seen as deserving of imperially sponsored defences and a substantial promotion in its ecclesiastical status by the emperor Anastasius I (491–518). According to the impressive inscription erected in the emperor's name, he had a city wall constructed and at the same time promoted the city to an archbishopric – although the first securely attested bishop was Epiphanius, who attended the sixth ecumenical council in Constantinople in 680, signing himself as bishop of the city of Euchaïta and bishop of the metropolis of Euchaïta.[62]

The exact point at which the defences were erected (or repaired) and at which the city became a bishopric in the first place remains contested.

---

59 See Haldon, Elton and Newhard 2015 and Bikoulis et al. 2015 for introductions to the archaeology of the region. For a detailed analysis of all relevant material, both textual and archaeological, see Haldon et al. forthcoming.

60 Laurent 1963, no. 852; *ZV* 1288 for seals of Peter, archbishop of Euchaïta, dated to the period ca. 700–750; *ZV* 1288 (650–730), seal of Peter of Euchaïta; 1287 (ca. 550–650), seal of Nicholas of Euchaïta; and 1289 (8th century) seal of Theodore of Euchaïta. See discussion in Walter 2003b: 51; Grotowski 2010: 93–94 with notes. *Pace* Walter 2003b: 51, however, these seals cannot be used to confirm the date of the miracles in Text 4 (*BHG* 1764), since the encomium that precedes them is clearly written, or more probably rewritten, by a tenth- or eleventh-century redactor. See discussion below on the texts.

61 Another, larger inscription, is to be seen in the grounds of the Çorum museum: see Grégoire 1909: 198–202; Anderson 1900: 156ff. The Beyözü fragment is smaller: Grégoire 1909: 212–213 (# 226); Anderson 1903: 12. For the bishop John, see Grégoire 1909: 213–214 (#227).

62 Darrouzès 1989: 215–221; Ohme 1990, 151 (no. 52); 292; *ACO* II, ii, 2. 786. 11; 894. 5.

Such walls were, of course, as much a symbol of urban status as they were efficacious, and, indeed, the later history of the city suggests, as we will see, that they were of limited defensive value. Without further archaeological work it is impossible to be precise, but it is possible that they pre-date Anastasius' work, which might thus have been a reconstruction or repair.

Its location distant from the imperial capital made Euchaïta, early in its history as a city, a place of internal banishment. The deposed patriarch of Antioch Peter the Fuller was sent there by the emperor Zeno in 476–477,[63] and its remoteness is suggested by the exile of the bishops Peter Mongus (482), Euphemius (496) and Macedonius (511: when the Sabir Huns threatened Euchaïta in 515, Macedonius fled to nearby Gangra), as well as others such as the archdeacon Liberatus, exiled there with his bishop Reparatus following the Three Chapters controversy in the middle of the sixth century. Certain heretics were either sent there or had settled there at some point during the tenth century.[64]

As far as its civic status is concerned,[65] Anastasius' elevation of Euchaïta to 'city' would, according to the inscription, have taken place in 515–518, the point at which the Sabir Huns were, or remained, a threat. But it remains unclear whether Euchaïta had achieved episcopal status before this time, so that Anastasius actually elevated it to an archbishopric. There is no mention of Euchaïta as a see at either the council of Chalcedon in 451 or in Pope Leo's Encyclical of 458.[66] Nevertheless, by the middle of the seventh century, according to an episcopal *notitia* of the period, it was twenty-eighth among the autocephalous archbishoprics[67] and, by the time Photios became patriarch in the ninth century, the see had

63 Theoph. 125.17–19; Malalas, xv, 380.23; see Kosiński 2010: 64–65.

64 Peter Mongus: Theoph. 130.12–13; Euphemius: Theoph., 140.19–20; Malalas xv: 400. 2 (Bonn); Theod. Lect., *HE*, ii, 15; Macedonius: Theoph. 155.22f; 156.9 (and 161.30); Theod. Lect., *HE*, ii, 36; Cedrenus, i, 634.3ff.); see also John Moschus, *Pratum Spirituale*, 2888D–2889A (cap. 38: trans. Wortley, p. 28). For the tenth century, see below.

65 The practice of associating a bishop with a city, and that each city should have its own bishop – although there were always exceptions – was confirmed by Zeno: *CJ* 1, 3.35 (36); cf. Darrouzès 1989.

66 For the different interpretations of the somewhat ambiguous evidence for the ecclesiastical status of Euchaïta, see Mango and Ševčenko 1972: 382–384 and Trombley 1985: 66 and 82, n. 8. The latter points out that the inscription merely records Anastasios' elevation of the city to archiepiscopal rank.

67 Darrouzès 1981: 8–9; Not. 1. 66 (206); for the date, see *PmbZ* #1531 and #1543; note also Jankowiak 2013: 438–448.

been promoted to metropolitan status, with four suffragan sees under its authority.[68]

It is possible that the wall(s) might also pre-date Anastasius' work (which should thus be seen as a reconstruction or repairing): Theophanes, or rather his source, merely reports that the Sabiri plundered Armenia, Cappadocia, Galatia and Pontus 'so as to stand near Euchaïta at a short distance'.[69] Since they did not take the city it may mean that it was already furnished with walls.[70] But at some time in the second half of the seventh century, almost certainly during the reign of Constans II, the city also had the promontory behind the urban centre furnished with defensive walls strong enough to dissuade any invaders from attacking. This area, referred to in the second collection of miracles as the 'strongholds' (*ochyromata*) or the 'fortress' (*kastron*), became the refuge for the population of the city during times of danger, and the miracles present a graphic account of the relationship between these defensive emplacements and the lower town. Archaeological survey has shown that the late Roman city was not large and is covered more or less entirely by the modern village, a settlement of some 130 dwellings, a mosque and a school. The church of St Theodore lay a short distance outside the Anastasian walls, which did not, however, completely encircle the town, merely running across the southern limits of the settlement to adjoin the high ground on either side. Associated with the structure that has been provisionally identified with this church are a number of other features, probably ancillary buildings associated with the pilgrim trade and possibly a monastic community, indicated by some of the surviving epigraphic material.[71]

The textual evidence suggests that the buildings associated with Theodore's cult – both the church and any other structures – were impressive; the church in particular is singled out as beautifully and lavishly decorated in both Gregory of Nyssa's late fourth-century homily and the miracle tales of Chrysippos, as well as in the later texts. The

---

68 See Darrouzès 1989: 215ff. for discussion; and 1981, 77–78; Not. 7. 686–690 (287) (a. 901–907); Not. 10. 668–672 (332) (mid-tenth century); older literature: Janin 1969: 148–155; Grumel–Darrouzès 1989: no. 527; Laurent 1963: 585ff.

69 Theoph. 161. 28–32. The Sabiri were an Oghur Turkic (or possibly Ugric) people inhabiting the region of modern Dagestan, to the west and north-west of the Caspian: see Sinor 1990. During the fifth century they were within the Hunnic confederacy, later under the Avars and eventually merged with the Khazars.

70 Trombley 1985: 75 and n. 28.

71 For a detailed account and presentation of the evidence see Haldon et al. forthcoming. For the church, see Bikoulis et al. 2015.

original church was destroyed in the Persian attack described in miracles 2 and 3 of the second collection and rebuilt soon after by bishop Eleutherios. Whether or not this building survived the Saracen attacks of the seventh century remains unclear, although both Persian and Arab raiders knew that the church would be a source of treasure – gold and silver liturgical vessels and plate, for example.[72] If Euchaïta did indeed benefit from the attention of John I Tzimiskes in the 970s, as is likely, then it may have been this church that was refurbished or rebuilt. That emperor certainly made substantial donations to other churches and to the Great Lavra on Mt Athos, as well as relaxing the legislation against endowing monastic houses with land that had been introduced by Nikephoros II Phokas a few years earlier.[73] His investment in the church of St Theodore at Euchaïta illustrates both the importance of the saint and his cult in the eyes of contemporaries as well as the centrality of imperial benefactions. That the town was prosperous, at least during the period of the various feasts and commemorative celebrations, bringing for a short time both wealth and people to Euchaïta, is confirmed by John Mauropous.[74]

The dramatically changed political–strategic situation after the middle of the seventh century gave Euchaïta a new importance in the overall strategic geography of the east Roman empire, located as it was a little to the north of one loop of the main route from Ankyra via Gangra to Amasia and onward, and not far from an important crossroads from which roads led south and south-east. With the important city of Amasia only a day's march to the east it now held a strategic value that it had not possessed hitherto. By the early ninth century it served as one of the bases of the Armeniakon forces, although it does not appear very often in accounts of imperial campaigns.[75] By the early tenth century, with the frontier now far away once more, its importance as a town must have depended almost entirely on the pilgrims who came to visit the shrine of St Theodore,

---

72 Mir. 10 (Delehaye 1909: 195.26–30); Mir. 9 (200. 3).

73 See the documents edited in Meyer 1894: 102–122.

74 De Lagarde 1882: no. 179 (pp. 122–123); no. 184 (pp. 162–163) and no. 189 (pp. 207–209); and cf. Delehaye 1909: 167. 14–17; and Karpozilos 1982: 42–43.

75 See Ramsay 1890: 197–221; with Bryer and Winfield 1985: 12–13; 20ff. Further on the Byzantine road system: Anderson 1897; Honigmann 1935; and the maps in Belke et al. 1984 and 1996. It is often assumed that Euchaita was the provincial or thematic military headquarters, because the general Leo (later Leo V) was intercepted near there in February 811 by Arab raiders, who were able to capture the military paychest, but Leo may well have been on his way to nearby Amasia, a much more imposing fortress and stronghold: see Theoph. 489. 17–21 (trans. Mango and Scott, 672); Brooks 1901: 76.

and, indeed, John Mauropous notes that it becomes a lovely place only during the festivals, emphasising otherwise its isolation and the poverty of the local economy and society. And in spite of its obvious importance as a centre for the honouring of St Theodore, Euchaïta appears only very occasionally in the *Lives* of saints – Lazaros of Galesion visited, as we have seen, and there are other very occasional mentions – but compared with several other such pilgrimage centres (such as that of St Michael at Germia, for example), which have named visitors, we know of hardly any individual visitors. Nor do we have much idea of how Euchaita related to neighbouring settlements and sites in terms of daily interactions, commerce or trade.

With the arrival of the Turks in the years after 1071 Euchaïta recedes once again into relative obscurity. Christian refugees are mentioned by John Mauropous in this period.[76] Whether or not the danger to the cult of Theodore the Recruit that the Türkmen raids posed was recognised must remain unknown.[77] Thereafter we hear of the see being transferred to the authority of the bishop of Kaisareia, but after the 1320s it disappears from the record, along with the local cult of St Theodore, whose relics had by then been dispersed and distributed among the faithful. Its replacement from the fourteenth century by a local Islamic cult bearing some similarities to that of Theodore is not untypical of Anatolia from this period on.[78] Euchaïta itself – known to Ottoman records from the sixteenth century and afterwards variously as Avkhat or Evhud – appears to have remained an occupied settlement throughout and until today, as the survival of its name suggests. The modern village of Beyözü is its direct descendant.

---

76 De Lagarde 1882: no. 180 (pp. 136–137).

77 See Grotowski 2010: 102, n. 150; de Lagarde 1882: no. 179 (p. 127), with pp. 11–12 above for the relics of Theodore *stratēlatēs*.

78 Pancaroğlu 2004: esp. 151–156.

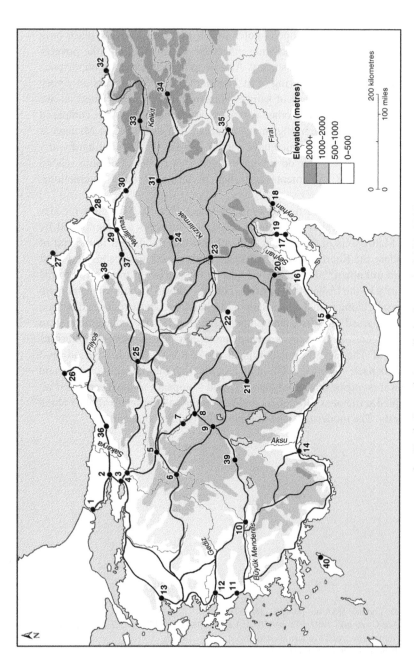

2   Euchaïta and Anatolia in the period 600–1100

Key to map: Euchaïta and Anatolia in the period 600–1100

Major towns or fortified centres

1	Chalcedon	2	Nikomedeia	3	Nikaia	4	Malagina	5	Dorylaion
6	Kotyaion	7	Kaborkion	8	Amorion	9	Akroinon	10	Chonai
11	Ephesos	12	Smyrna	13	Adramyttion	14	Attaleia	15	Seleukeia
16	Tarsos	17	Anazarbos	18	Germanikeia	19	Sision	20	Podandos
21	Ikonion	22	Koron	23	Kaisareia	24	Charsianon	25	Ankyra
26	Amastris	27	Sinope	28	Amisos	29	Amasia	30	Dazimon
31	Sebasteia	32	Trapezous	33	Koloneia	34	Kamacha	35	Melitene
36	Klaudiopolis	37	Euchaïta	38	Gangra	39	Sozopolis	40	Rhodes

River names

Modern	Ancient/Medieval
Sakarya	Sangarios
Yeşilirmak	Iris
Kızılırmak	Halys
Büyük Menderes	Maeander
Şeyhan	Saros
Firat	Euphrates
Filyos	Billaios
Kelkit	Lykos
Gediz	Hermos
Aksu	Eurymedon
Ceyhan	Pyramos

2

THE TEXTS

Context: martyrdoms and miracles

The genres within which the collections of miracles and the martyr
accounts of the two Theodores belong need little comment here, having
been well studied in respect of their evolution as well as in terms of style,
literary affiliation and periodisation.[1] Of the numerous versions of the
martyrdoms, we shall be dealing with four of Theodore 'the Recruit' and
one of Theodore 'the General'. These are, for Theodore 'the Recruit': *BHG*
1765c, composed by Chrysippos of Jerusalem (fl. ca. 408–479) in that city,
edited and published separately by both Delehaye and by Sigalas (Text 1),
a text that also includes twelve miracles of the saint;[2] *BHG* 1761 (Text 2),
composed probably between the early sixth and early seventh century;[3]
BHG 1765 (Text 3), probably composed in the tenth century;[4] and *BHG*
1764 (Text 4), certainly an eleventh-century work comprising much earlier
material, including eight miracle stories that can be dated to the seventh
century.[5] For Theodore 'the General', for whom also a number of versions
of his martyrdom exist, we will take *BHG* 1752 (Text 5), a metaphrastic
account of the later tenth century.[6] These texts served as exemplars for
later writers and hagiographers of the two Theodores and formed a key
element in the standard repertoire of eastern saints' passions.[7]

The two sets of miracle tales for Theodore 'the Recruit' are both

1 See, most recently, and with further literature: Pratsch 2005; Detoraki 2014;
Efthymiadis 2014b; and esp. Déroche 1993; for broader context also Hinterberger 2014a;
2014b; Talbot 2008; Browning 1981. Discussion of narrative structure in hagiographical
writing more generally: Rapp 1998; and for a catalogue and presentation of Byzantine
miracle collections: Efthymiadis 1999 with the analysis of the genre in Pratsch 2005.

2 Sigalas 1921: 51–79; Delehaye 1925a: 55–72.

3 Delehaye 1909: 127–135; 1925a: 29–39.

4 Sigalas 1925: 225–226.

5 Delehaye 1909: 183–201; 1925a: 49–55.

6 Delehaye 1909: 168–182.

7 See esp. Antonopoulou 2009.

attached to a version of the martyrdom, although a number of the miracles from the Chrysippos collection circulated independently and in different hagiographical contexts. The tradition of these miracles seems to have taken two different routes, resulting in two quite separate collections. An earlier group, compiled by the later fifth century at the latest, consists of a group of eleven or twelve miracles, of varying length and detail, and appears to have been very popular and had widespread currency in the Byzantine world – the manuscript tradition stretches from the tenth to the sixteenth century. These are first attested as part of the encomium composed by the presbyter Chrysippos of Jerusalem, a disciple of Euthymios the Great in his community in the Judaean desert, founded in 428/429 (Text 1).[8] They were probably delivered to an audience of monks and/or churchmen sometime between 455 and 479,[9] during Chrysippos' service as presbyter and then *staurophylax* in the church of the Anastasis in Jerusalem. This collection also circulated independently by the later fifth century and possibly earlier, although it is impossible to say whether Chrysippos was responsible for the collection in the first place (*BHG* 1765f),[10] and, along with a number of other miracles ascribed to Theodore – that of the *kolyva*, for example (see below), and that of Theodore and the dragon – seems to represent the main tradition.[11]

The other group consists of eight miracles (although there may originally have been ten) and represents an entirely independent tradition compiled originally at some time in the second half of the seventh century (Text 4).[12] The earliest surviving version was probably redacted in the eleventh century. It is an unusual collection insofar as it represents a particular moment in the history of seventh-century Byzantium and more particularly of the city of Euchaïta and the situation in which such

8 *CPG* III, 6706. Chrysippos was presbyter of the church of the Anastasis from ca. 456, then *staurophylax* from ca. 466 until his death in 479: see Di Berardino 2006: 251–252; Efthymiadis et al. 2011: 68; Flusin 2011: 201. For the encomium: Sigalas 1921 (text at 51–79); 1937: 81–93; Delehaye 1925a: 55–72.

9 See Sigalas 1937: 88–89. The few details we have of Chrysippos' career are provided in Cyril of Skythopolis' *Vita Euthymii* (*BHG* 647–648; *CPG* 7535), ed. Schwartz 1939: 280, s.v. Χρύσιππος.

10 Edited in Sigalas 1924: 310–339 (text); slightly different version in Delehaye 1925a: 60–71. See *BHG* 1765b, d, h–v.

11 *BHG* 1766 (see Delehaye 1925a: 15 and 46–49), 1766a–h, 1767, 1767k, 1768–1769. Further discussion of the tale of Theodore and the dragon: Delehaye 1909: 37–39; 1925: 14–15; text: 46–48.

12 Ed. Delehaye 1909: 183–201; and 1925: 49–55. See Efthymiadis 2011b: 98.

provincial settlements found themselves in the period from the Persian wars in the 620s up to the Arab raids and attacks in the second half of the seventh century. These miracle stories reflect a strongly local tradition, and in many respects offer parallels to collections of miracles for local Constantinopolitan saints or from other cities of the same period, such as those of Cosmas and Damian, Artemius or Therapon.[13] The two collections have no miracles in common and thus appear to reflect two very different milieux for their composition, the earlier group (probably) set in Euchaïta, although perhaps reflecting life in a larger urban centre: the town in which the stories take place is in fact never named, but the account was certainly written in Jerusalem.[14] The later collection appears to have been composed by a writer in Euchaïta itself, drawing upon local tales and orally transmitted accounts as its source. By the eleventh century, however, the two collections are found side by side in a single manuscript (cod. Vind. theol. gr. 60, fol. 259–270 [Text 4] and 270–280 [Text 1]), although the version of the martyrdom in the Chrysippos encomium (Text 1) in the manuscript is missing, presumably – as Sigalas surmised – because the story is told in even greater detail in the immediately preceding text.[15] Yet no text is extant in which the two collections of miracles are integrated, and it is likely, therefore, that they always remained separate. There are other examples where parallel traditions of *Lives* and/or *Miracles* of a saint existed side by side – as with the evolution of the collection of miracles of St Thekla, for example.[16] While the date at which the different versions of the *Vita* and martyrdom came into existence cannot be determined with precision, the later collection of miracles (in our Text 4) can be anchored historically from internal evidence, while the earlier collection can be dated very approximately from both internal and external evidence, as we shall see.

---

13 On these other collections and the issue of their largely local focus, see below.

14 While Chrysippos appears deliberately to avoid naming names and places (except in miracle 12, and indirectly in miracle 1), in his introductory laudation he notes that there is no church for St Theodore yet in his day in Jerusalem (Sigalas 1921: 51.17–18; Delehaye 1925a: 55 [1]. 23–24), whereas in the miracle stories that follow the church of the saint is a central focus for much of the action, suggesting Euchaïta as the obvious location.

15 From 51.25 to 58.1. See Sigalas 1921: 25.

16 See *Miracles of St Thekla*: x–xiii.

The martyrdom accounts: date and development

Before examining the miracle collections in more detail it will be helpful to consider the text(s) of the *Passio* or *Vita* that frequently accompany the miracle collections.[17] As is usual with such accounts, the extent to which any of the details other than the martyr's name reflect actual historical events remains entirely unknown and, as Delehaye and many others have noted, the considerable number of common features shared by a wide range of such martyrologies means that attempts to establish a kernel of fact must be doomed to failure.[18] The texts associated with Theodore represent a long evolution across several centuries and all conform to the well-established pattern that began with the first accounts of martyrdoms from the second century.[19] But, as we shall see, it is possible to note some significant changes in style and format across the several versions of the martyrdom, changes that offer some credible evidence for an approximate date of composition, or at least redaction, of the texts in question.

Like many other martyrdom accounts, the martyrdom stories for Theodore the Recruit have a number of topoi in common and, as Delehaye pointed out,[20] it is dangerous to assume any historicity in the details of these tales, even if it is sometimes possible to isolate possible contexts and sources for particular motifs, as we shall see below. The oldest version of the *Passio* is represented in the encomium ascribed to Gregory of Nyssa, already mentioned (*BHG* 1760).[21] According to this, Theodore was of noble birth and born in the east, was recruited into the infantry and during the reign of Maximian (286–305 in the west) came to the region of Amasia with his unit, which was to take up winter quarters there. When the persecution began Theodore was forced to confess his Christian faith. After an initial

17 Discussion and presentation of the mss: Delehaye 1925a: 11–17; and for the ways in which Byzantine hagiographers combined different sub-genres – bringing together a *vita* with a collection of miracles, for example, or a *passio*, an encomium and some miracles – see Hinterberger 2014a: 41–49.

18 E.g. Delehaye 1909: 111–119.

19 See Quasten 1950: 176–185.

20 Delehaye 1909: 111–113, 118.

21 *CPG* II, 3183. Partial ed. Delehaye 1925a: 27–29; Cavarnos 1990: 61–71; trans. Leemans 2003: 83–91. While there was some debate about this attribution, this is now generally accepted. See Altenburger and Mann 1988: 297. The homily was delivered in Euchaïta in either 379 or 380: Daniélou 1955; most recently and persuasively Zuckerman 1991: 479–486 with literature. For discussion of the homily in the context of the saint's annual *panēgyris*, see Limberis 2011: esp. 55–63.

interrogation he was released in the hope that he would reconsider, but he exploited this opportunity to set fire to the temple of Cybele, the mother of Gods, in Amasia.[22] He was subsequently arrested again and tried, but remained steadfast in spite of threats and promises, along with bribes in gold, dignities and priestly office. Eventually he was tortured by having his flesh torn, imprisoned, interrogated once more and, finally, condemned to be burned.

Gregory's account lacks many of the details found in what later became the established tale of Theodore's martyrdom – notably the tale of St Theodore and the dragon and of the pious lady Eusebia. Neither do these episodes appear in the account in the encomium written by Chrysippos of Jerusalem (*BHG* 1765c, Text 1), although indirect reference is made to Eusebia at the end of the martyrdom story. The latter survives in whole or in part in several manuscripts of the tenth to the sixteenth centuries.[23] In rhetorical structure and language it follows fairly closely Gregory of Nyssa's encomium, and there is no reason to doubt that, in composing it, Chrysippos had Gregory's homily in mind or before him. The text is written in a relatively high style, but is less accomplished as a whole than a comparable fifth-century and almost contemporary composition, the *Miracles of St Thekla*.[24] In the course of the introductory section the author informs us that there was at this time no church in Jerusalem dedicated to Theodore,[25] a mention that raises the question of the occasion for the composition of the encomium. Sigalas argued for an earlier date, in the 450s, on the grounds that the wording used by Chrysippos himself in the prologue and in the epilogue to the encomium, preceding the twelve miracles, reflects the sentiments of a less experienced speaker who is aware of his shortcomings (see, for example, Sigalas 1921: 51. 4–16; 78.13–79.4), and thus was written shortly after he became a priest in the church of the Anastasis in Jerusalem in 455, a suggestion which has some merit.[26] In miracle 12 a great fire in

22 For the cult of Cybele see Mitchell 1993: 19–22; Beard 1994; Vermaseren 1977. The cult of Cybele as mother goddess evolved in Anatolia and then spread westwards with Greek colonists and later to Rome, becoming associated with the divinities Rhea, Demeter and Gaia.

23 Detailed discussion in Sigalas 1921: 18–31, with analysis of the interrelationships between them at 31–49 (stemma at 48). Sigalas later revised some of his conclusions: 1937: 89–93.

24 See Efthymiadis et al. 2011: 67–68; and *Miracles of St Thekla*: viii–xii.

25 Sigalas 1921: 51. 2 and 17–18.

26 Sigalas 1921: 4. He also suggested that the collection must have a *terminus post quem* of the year 452, in which Sphorakios became consul, since he is mentioned with this title in

Constantinople is reported and, although there were several fires in the city during the middle decades of the century (notably in 461 as well as 464/5 and 478),[27] it has generally been considered that the great fire of 464/5 is meant, thus excluding a date of composition of Chrysippos' text before this point. In fact, while the fire of 464 is well documented (even if there are discrepancies in the dating because of contradictions between sources), an earlier fire, perhaps that of 461, is entirely possible.[28]

In this connection it is worth recalling that the empress (Aelia) Eudocia, the wife of Theodosius II, had been in the Holy Land since the mid-440s; indeed, it was she who had encouraged the bishop Juvenalis to consecrate Chrysippos and his brother Gabriel priests, in the year 455.[29] Chrysippos, as we have seen, served in the church of the Anastasis (becoming *staurophylax* in 467), while Gabriel was named abbot of the monastery of St Stephen the protomartyr in Jerusalem by the empress herself. Eudocia died in Jerusalem in 460. Eudocia's granddaughter, likewise Eudocia, also spent a short while in Jerusalem in about 471–472, where she died soon after her arrival, having previously spent some sixteen years in semi-captivity at the court of the Vandal kings in Africa with her mother and her sister Placidia.[30] Given the very specific reference in his introductory remarks to the absence of a church for St Theodore in Jerusalem, the question arises as to whether the encomium may not have been intended as an appeal to one of these female members of the imperial family to endow such a church. It is interesting to note that Chrysippos himself compares Theodore favourably, in the account of his martyrdom, with St Stephen (Sigalas 1921: 55. 16); that Aelia Eudocia certainly had a particular relationship with the protomartyr, endowing his church in Jerusalem as well as supporting the monastery dedicated in his name in the same city; and that Eudocia, the granddaughter, was (probably) buried in Jerusalem in the church of St Stephen alongside her grandmother.

We may also note that a now lost inscription from Saframbolu in northern Turkey, reported in the later nineteenth century, purported to describe the donation of a church of St Stephen by the same empress (Aelia) Eudocia, along with the relic of the protomartyr's foot, to 'the city of Theodore'

---

miracle 12. But individuals retained the honorific title of consul after the year during which they held the office, so this does not help date the miracle.

27 See Schneider 1941: 383–384. For the fires: Janin 1964: 35–36.

28 For the date: Whitby and Whitby 1989: 87, n. 285; Mango 1986b: 25–28.

29 For Eudocia: *PLRE* 2:408–409 (Aelia Eudocia 2).

30 See *PLRE* 2: 407–408 (Eudocia 1).

(probably Euchaïta, from where the inscription may originally have been taken) as a gesture of thanks for her recovery, attributed to the protomartyr, from an accident suffered while visiting the Holy Land.[31] While the authenticity of the inscription can no longer be established with certainty, if the reading is correct it would lend support, if such were needed, to the role of Euchaïta as a significant centre by the 430s, along with Aelia Eudocia's interest in both Stephen the protomartyr and Theodore the recruit.[32]

Since Eudocia died in 460, however, and since it is the fire of 464/465 that is referred to in miracle 12 of the Chrysippos encomium, this renders Sigalas' original idea that the text dates to before 460 unlikely, since Eudocia's death cannot be reconciled with the date of the fires of either 461 or 464/465. There is little doubt that the composition of the text is unitary – the twelve miracles are clearly built into the rhetorical structure of the whole (see Chrysippos' concluding comment on the number 12) – so a date of writing prior to 461, or during Eudocia's final years, has to be excluded. On the other hand, and as noted above, Aelia Eudocia's granddaughter was in Jerusalem in 471–472. There was an established tradition among the female members of her family of endowing churches.[33] Apart from the churches mentioned already – that of St Polyeuktos, endowed by her grandmother, and that of St Euphemia, endowed by her mother Eudoxia – her sister Placidia also endowed the church of St Euphemia in Constantinople.[34] It is entirely possible that, like her grandmother before her, the younger Eudocia also favoured the cult of the two martyrs Stephen and Theodore. Hypothetical though this construct is, it may lend some support to the idea that Chrysippos was appealing to Eudocia directly in his encomium, and thus might, perhaps, suggest a date between 465 and 472 for the composition of Chrysippos' encomium, perhaps in 471–472 after her arrival in the city. Requests for support for church-building or endowments were, after all, not unusual, as the example in the *Life* of Porphyry of Gaza testifies.[35]

Chrysippos' text includes the accounts of the burning of the temple and of the angelic choir in the prison, but it introduces a new element: a

---

31 Doublet 1889: 294–299, text and translation of the inscription at 294.

32 For Eudocia in the Holy Land see Lenski 2004: 117–118 with further literature and sources.

33 See Holum 1982.

34 *PLRE* 2: 887 (Placidia 1). See *Greek Anthology*, i, 10. 20–33 and 12. 14–17; also *PLRE* 2: 636 (Anicia Iuliana 3).

35 *Vita Porphyrii Gazensis*: caps. 42 and 53 (and see Barnes 2010: 260–283). For the activities of Aelia Eudocia in Jerusalem, see Holum 1982: 217–220.

story about how, on the way to his execution, the saint drives off through his prayers an infestation of demons (in the form of snakes) – an occasion which, the text states, was the reason for the construction of a church in the saint's name.[36] Whether this tale was in fact at the root of the story of how the saint killed the dragon that had infested the area around Euchaïta remains unclear.

Chrysippos' encomium makes reference for the first time to the pious woman who preserved the saint's remains and laid them to rest in a tomb on her own property, where later the church was built, and, while not naming her explicitly, indicates that she was already known as Eusebia:

> she who came into possession of the remains of those holy bones, distributing money in plenty to the watchmen so that she could store these unspeakable riches as a treasure in her own house. *She is pious in name and in purpose,*[37] worthy to be ranked with Mary, worthy to be counted with Salome and to be mentioned alongside Susannah – the unguents were brought to the life-giving tomb by them. The house itself was chosen by her as a tomb for the martyr, and the same gift was also assigned by her later as the place for the very first church and atrium. For in her stead this noble martyr came to be established as owner and protector of the whole place.[38]

While this account seems to be the first to make mention of these particular acts, it reflects a well-established tradition in which pious women rescue a martyr's remains and lay them to rest. One may ask whether the introduction of Eusebia, perhaps as a role model, may not be understood as an appeal to the younger Eudocia for support for building a church for St Theodore.[39] This motif was also one aspect of a tradition that can be followed back into the fourth century whereby individuals competed for the honour of housing or accommodating in some other way either a living holy man or the relics of a saint or martyr on their own property. At the end of the fourth century the aristocrats Saturninus and Victor competed for the presence of the monk Isaac, each building a monastery for him on their own estate. While Saturninus was apparently successful, since a substantial monastic establishment developed on his land, Isaac was ultimately buried on the estate of yet another local aristocrat, a certain Aurelianus. This phenomenon becomes especially obvious in the fifth and

---

36 Sigalas 1921: 58.15–59.4.
37 Greek εὐσεβής (*eusebēs*), pious; εὐσέβεια (*eusebeia*), piety.
38 Sigalas 1921: 57. 9–17.
39 I am indebted to Claudia Rapp for this suggestion.

sixth centuries. The competition among local cities for the body of Symeon the Stylite after his death in 459 is a more extreme example, since the remains needed a military guard to protect them on their way to Antioch; while rivalry among senior members of the establishment (Gelanius, a local landowner, the former praetorian prefect Cyrus and the empress Eudoxia) for the presence of Daniel the Stylite on their estates – through the raising of competing pillars for him – was fierce. The encomium by Chrysippos represents another illustration of this motif.[40]

Other extant versions of the life and martyrdom of Theodore built upon these beginnings. The next stage may be represented by a somewhat more developed and much longer account (Text 2: *BHG* 1761 [–1762d]), variations on which are found in several manuscript versions, of which Delehaye took two for his edition – Paris. gr.1470, a. 890 and Paris. gr. 520, 11th c. (= *BHG* 1762d)[41] – and in which several details of the saint's companions during his military service are changed or expanded. As Delehaye noted, the details given in the different versions in the mss vary in respect of the names of the characters involved and a number of other minor features, a typical feature of such texts.[42] In this version the reigning emperors are explicitly mentioned as Maximian and Maximinus, and we learn that Theodore was recruited into the legion of the Marmaritai, based at Amasia, by its commander Bringas. The narrative of Theodore's fight with the dragon now appears for the first time: some four miles from the city of Euchaïta there was a wood, where dwelt a dragon that had been terrorising the region. It happened that one day Theodore was passing along the road and, spying the dragon, he attacked it in the name of Christ and slew it. When some time afterwards Theodore was required to sacrifice to the pagan gods by Bringas, he refused. He was questioned by a *ducenarius* by the name of Poseidonius, and then allowed some time to consider his position, during which period he bolstered the faith of other Christians he knew and also set fire to the temple of the mother of gods. He was then accused by a certain Kronides and taken before the judge, named as Publius Straton. Failing to persuade Theodore to change his mind about sacrificing, the judge condemned him to solitary confinement until he should starve. But in the

40 For Saturninus and Victor: *Vita Isaacii* 4. 14; 4. 18. See Barnes 2010: 242–246; also Bowes 2008: 114; the body of Symeon the Stylite: Evagrius, *HE* 1. 13 (trans. Whitby 2000: 36–38); and competition over Daniel the Stylite: *Vita Danielis Stylitae*, caps. 29–35 (trans. Dawes and Baynes 1948: 24–28).
41 Ed. Delehaye 1909: 127–135; 1925a: 29–39; Starck 1912; see Delehaye 1925a: 12–13.
42 Delehaye 1909: 22–23.

night, when Christ had appeared to Theodore and promised to support him, the saint, accompanied by angels, began to chant. When his gaolers saw this they hurriedly brought him bread and water, but he rejected these and would not touch them. There followed a second interrogation and, failing yet again to persuade him, the judge ordered his torture by means of iron hooks ripping his skin. Following a final attempt to convert him, Theodore was at last condemned to death by burning. The executioners collect firewood from workshops and bath-houses and build a pyre. Theodore then strips off his clothing and attempts to remove his footwear, but his friends rush in to help him. He refuses the nails that were to fix him to the stake or cross, and once bound and standing at the stake the saint utters a long prayer. When he notices one of his fellow soldiers, Kleonikos, among the crowd, he urges him to persevere. As the pyre is lit the flames envelope the martyr like a veil, and his soul rises up to heaven like a flash of lightning. Finally, a pious woman named Eusebia recovers the body of the saint.

Most of this account follows the story of the saint's martyrdom as retailed in the homily of Gregory of Nyssa, while the final sections are borrowed from the passion of St Polycarpus, one of the best-known early Christian martyr accounts – the passage about the martyr rejecting the use of nails because God would enable him to endure the fire without being secured, for example.[43] More importantly, it was long ago demonstrated that the martyrdom of St Theagenes, which survives only in a Latin version and which was in circulation by the eighth century, is clearly derived in large part from this account of the passion of St Theodore. The episode of the dragon is not found in the Theagenes text and in only one of the extant versions of this Theodore passion, and Delehaye and others have argued persuasively, in light of the awkward way in which it appears to be inserted into the text at the end of the opening section, that this was a later interpolation. Delehaye also argued this view on the grounds that corroborative evidence for the dragon story does not appear until much later.[44]

---

43 See *Acta Polycarpi* 13. 3 (320); Quasten 1950: 76–82; Delehaye 1925a: 13; and see Ronchey 1990, and Barnes 2010: 367–378.

44 See especially Franchi de Cavalieri 1909/1912, followed by Delehaye 1909: 23–25; the dragon-slaying is present in cod. Paris. Gr. 1470 but not in the eleventh-century Paris gr. 520. See Delehaye 1909: 127. 12 and note; 1925: 13; and Hengstenberg 1912/1913 for a detailed discussion of all the versions of the dragon-slaying miracle. By the eleventh century we may assume that both versions existed in parallel, just as two versions of the life and passion of St Theodore the General were current, one with the dragon and Eusebia, the other without: see below.

But, as we have seen, the archaeological and material cultural evidence shows that the dragon was associated with Theodore certainly by the seventh century and possibly by the later fifth or early sixth century (see above, pp. 4–5 and 12). A possible *terminus ante quem* for this text may be offered by the hymn to Theodore the Recruit ascribed to Theodore of Stoudios, who was certainly familiar with the story of Theodore slaying a dragon in the early ninth century. The short verse account of the martyrdom he composed follows the account in Chrysippos (Text 1), but, as in Text 2, includes at the beginning the story of the dragon. Theodore also used the image of the flames of the martyr's pyre forming an arch (a motif drawn from the *Acta Polycarpi* 15. 2), although it is possible that Theodore himself introduced these elements and that Text 2 post-dates Theodore's hymn.[45] In either case, though, the dragon was apparently a well-known motif by the early ninth century.

We may therefore agree with Delehaye's judgment that the dragon-slaying passage is probably an addition, interpolated somewhat clumsily near the beginning of a version of the martyrdom which came into existence after the encomium of Chrysippos, and from which the Theagenes text was then developed. But this addition was clearly much earlier than Delehaye thought, so that although the earliest manuscript witness to this version (Text 2) dates to the year 890, as noted (Paris. gr. 1470),[46] in its original form (without the dragon) it is probably a product of the sixth century, perhaps even the late fifth century. In favour of the sixth is the reference to 'the city of Euchaïta',[47] which, if we can place any reliance on the use of the term *polis*, might well suggest a date of composition after the first decade of that century, when the town first formally acquired that status (see above, p. 14).[48] This is also the first occasion on which the pious woman Eusebia is mentioned specifically (rather than indirectly, as in Chrysippos' text), appearing by name, in this case at the end of the story, where she is referred to simply as 'a certain Eusebia, aptly-named in view of her pious life', who placed the body in a tomb at her home at Euchaïta, in the metropolitan see of Amasia, where she also commemorated his passing (and, according to a

---

45 Pitra 1876: 362. γ; 364. δ and compare with Delehaye 1909: 134.24. Pitra retained the incorrect attribution to Theodore *Stratēlatēs* given in the ms, but the text quite clearly refers to the miracles and the martyrdom of Theodore the Recruit as recounted by Chrysippos.

46 See Delehaye 1909: 121–122.

47 Ed. Delehaye 1909: 127. 11–12.

48 Delehaye 1909: 21–25.

variant version, constructed a *martyrion*) and 'where his commemoration takes place today'.[49]

At some point during the second half of the tenth century the earlier text was reworked, and variants of this revised metaphrastic version of the martyrdom (*BHG* 1763) are preserved in a number of other manuscripts used by Delehaye for his edition: codd. Paris. gr. 789 and 1450 (11th c.), cod. Paris. gr. 1529, and cod. Vat. gr. 1245 (both 12th c.). The menologion of the Metaphrast is, of course, widely represented in the ms tradition, so that there are many versions of this particular account.[50] In this variant the story of the dragon is introduced a little more subtly (although it is omitted altogether from the version in cod. Paris. gr. 1450), and for the first time the lady Eusebia now appears as the owner of the property where the dragon lurks. Here she is described as 'one of the distinguished and notable' people of the region, who possessed the property as a paternal inheritance,[51] and she begs the martyr to leave the area because of the awful fate that had befallen others who had dared to approach the dragon. The passage dealing with the deposition at Euchaïta of the martyr's remains is very similar to that of the older text discussed above, although a little more elaborate in detail and descriptive language. This version ends with a long 'historical' section on the role of Constantine I in the establishment and safeguarding of Christianity, the impact of the apostate Julian and the story of the *kollyba*.[52] Both in style and presentation this account reflects the changes

49 Ed. Delehaye 1909: 135, n. 18; 1925: 39.

50 Ed. Delehaye 1909: 136–150; 1925: 39–45. The metaphrastic origins of the text were clearly demonstrated by Delehaye 1897; see Starck 1912. For versions with and without the dragon story, see Delehaye 1909: 26; 1925a: 13. On Symeon Metaphrastes and the metaphrastic movement more broadly, see Høgel 2014.

51 Delehaye 1909: 137.19; 137.29–138.1.

52 For this well-known story, which appears in a number of manuscripts, see Petit 1898–1899; Delehaye 1925a: 21–22; Cozza-Luzi, in *NPB* x, 2: 138–143. The miracle is recounted in a text spuriously ascribed to the patriarch Nektarios (*BHG* 1768; *CPG* II, 4300), and repeated thereafter by many writers (*BHG* 1768a–d, 1769). According to the tradition, Julian was aware that Christians would be hungry after the first week of Lenten fasting, and would buy food in the marketplaces on Saturday. He ordered that blood from pagan sacrifices be sprinkled on the food that was sold there, thus making it unsuitable as Lenten fare, or indeed as food for Christians at all. But St Theodore appeared in a dream to the bishop, warning him that the people should not eat food bought at the marketplace that day, but only *kollyba*, boiled wheat. This term was purportedly new to the bishop, and Theodore explained that this was the term used locally (around Euchaïta). It may, of course, seem somewhat unlikely that the bishop was unfamiliar with the term, since it derived from aG *kollybos*, a small coin, in a neut. pl. form *kollyba*, also meaning small round cakes; it was

that affected middle Byzantine hagiographical writing from the middle of the ninth century onwards, as both the nature of the authors of such works and the social milieu from which they came changed substantially. This is marked in particular by a tendency to an increasingly sophisticated style and language aimed at a culturally more sophisticated and more literate audience.[53]

A very much shorter account, but which makes reference to some of the traditional details, is represented by the short text *BHG* 1765 (Text 3).[54] According to this version the saint's remains were taken after his death by 'certain devout men' and laid to rest in Amasia. We learn the names of the saint's father and mother (Erythraios and Polyxene) and that after his wife's death, following the birth of Theodore, Erythraios invented a means of suckling the infant with a glass bottle. We also learn the names of the saint's teacher, Proclus, and of the Christian, Helladius, who persuaded him of his Christian mission. At the end of the account we are told that an argument between men from Amasia and men from Euchaïta broke out about where the saint's remains should be interred. The 'brethren' from Euchaïta argued that they should be taken thither, because that is what the saint had ordained before his death.[55] The writer adds that he is not sure of the outcome of this disagreement, and that he had composed his text for a person of considerable spiritual authority. The whole episode recalls the fifth- and sixth-century competition to win the relics and actual person of a saint or holy person for one's own estate or property alluded to already, although it seems that such rivalries continued into the middle Byzantine period.

The origins of the short *vita* in particular are difficult to discern – the final statement regarding the disagreement between the people of Amasia and those of Euchaïta about where the saint's remains should be interred might suggest a time at which monastic communities already existed in both places, and this is most unlikely to have been the case for Euchaïta

---

commonly eaten by monks. See Lampe 1961, s.v. *kollyba*; *ODB* 2: 1137–1138; also Dawes and Baynes, in *Vita Theod. Syk.*, comm. to §6 (90; 186). As a result, the first Saturday of Great Lent has come to be known as 'Theodore Saturday' in the Orthodox churches. Further on the history of this particular tale, see Efthymiadis 2011c.

53 See, in particular, Hinterberger 2014b: 226–228, 238; Efthymiadis and Kalogeras 2014: 252, 261–266.

54 Sigalas 1925: 225–226; 1937: 99–102; Delehaye 1925a: 45–46; discussion of mss Sigalas 1925: 222; Delehaye 1925a: 14 [11] – [12].

55 Sigalas 1925: 226.21–23.

before the saint's cult was well established there. On the other hand, vague descriptive terms of address such as 'brethren' or 'fathers' might just as easily include lay as well as monastic or ecclesiastical personnel, so this does not get us very far.[56] That this might reflect a real disagreement between two monastic communities at the time the account was written down remains an intriguing possibility, given the fact that Theodore was associated with both places from the beginning (as far as the evidence permits us to say). But this brief account makes no reference to the saint's burning down of the temple in Amasia nor to the saint's chanting accompanied by heavenly voices while in his cell.

Delehaye dismissed this text as a later hagiographical invention designed to fill in some gaps about the saint's infancy, since abridgments and curtailed or summarised versions of both miracle tales and martyrdom stories were certainly recognised features of tenth-century and later collections. This view has generally been followed by later commentators, and is indeed the most likely explanation, since such 'lives before the martyrdom' are not found before the tenth century.[57] Yet, it ignores the burning of the pagan temple, and it might seem somewhat unlikely that a later hagiographer would expect his version to be taken seriously were he to compose a story purporting to represent the saint's early years and passion that ignored entirely some of the saint's most famous acts, so one wonders why the author did not employ all the traditional motifs. Nevertheless, and in light of the reasons enumerated by Delehaye, Sigalas's categorical affirmation of it as the earliest extant account of the martyrdom seems less than wholly persuasive, even if an early date in this particular instance should not be entirely excluded.[58] At the least, this short life probably pre-dates those presented in the encomium of Nikephoros Ouranos (*BHG* 1762m) and in our Text 4 (*BHG* 1764), discussed below, and may lie at some point behind their shared model. While the latter include details such as the names of the martyr's parents, they also both omit details found in this brief version (such as the names of the martyr's teacher Proclus and spiritual father Helladius); and they both also include details not found in it – such as the name of the *praepositus* Bringas and the governor Publius Straton. It thus seems likely that at least one more version of a 'Life before

56 See Efthymiadis and Kalogeras 2014: 249.

57 Delehaye 1909: 33; 1921: 24–27; Halkin 1962: 310; Walter 2003b: 45, n. 7. On the work of later writers in abridging and restyling earlier material, see Detoraki 2014: 64–72 with further literature; note also Caseau 2009: 612–164 and Hinterberger 2014a: 41–49.

58 Sigalas 1937: 100–102.

the martyrdom' existed, one that included both information provided on the saint's infancy and early years as well as that found in, for example, the metaphrastic version, but that is no longer extant.

The encomium written by Nikephoros Ouranos has already been mentioned.[59] It was also included in the now-lost cod. Taurinensis C.IV.18, along with our Text 4 (*BHG* 1764) and a number of other versions of the Theodore martyrdom and miracles, although the only extant version of the Ouranos text is now in a thirteenth-century Athonite codex.[60] This encomium includes the details of Theodore's birth and childhood set out in the short 'Life before the martyrdom' (Text 3, *BHG* 1765), but follows the metaphrastic version (*BHG* 1763) in introducing the dragon story, linking it to the presence of the lady Eusebia and including after the account of the passion the miracle of the *kolyba*/κόλυβα (the word can be spelled with a single or a double 'l'). Also, and as in both *BHG* 1761 (Text 2) and the metaphrastic version (*BHG* 1763), the governor or magistrate of Amasia is named as Publius Straton (although in the latter he is simply 'Pouplios'). In *BHG* 1764 (Text 4) he is not named at all.

Significantly, however, in Ouranos' version Eusebia has been raised to senatorial rank, is now related to the emperors Maximianus and Maximinus[61] and is the owner of the place where the dragon had dwelt. Ouranos' account of the martyrdom thereafter is essentially the same as in *BHG* 1764 – most emphasis is placed on the account of the martyr's meeting with Eusebia and his subsequent slaying of the dragon, with a relatively brief summary of the trial and martyrdom. At the end of the account of Theodore's death Ouranos includes the story of the saint's appearance before the painter who was to portray him for Eusebia, and follows this with the account of the apostate Julian's attempt to trick Christians into eating food defiled by sacrifice and the story of the *kolyba*. None of the 'historical' miracles about Euchaïta to be found in Text 4 are included, while in Text 4 itself the miracle of the *kolyba* does not appear and the story of the image is presented as the first of the enumerated miracles.

Halkin proposed that Ouranos and the author of *BHG* 1764, both writing in the late tenth or very early eleventh century, used a common source, but that each chose to conclude the account differently.[62] This common source in turn appears to have derived some of its information from a tradition

---

59 Ed. Halkin 1962.
60 Cod. Athonensi Stauronicetae 18, ff. 93–98.
61 Ed. Halkin 1962: 316 §7.
62 Halkin 1962: 311–313.

represented in the short 'life before the martyrdom' discussed above (Text 3: *BHG* 1765).[63]

The version of the *passio* that accompanied the second collection of miracles (*BHG* 1764) is almost certainly a redacted version of a somewhat later composition.[64] It survives in a twelfth-century manuscript, Vindob. theologicus gr. 60, fol. 259–270, which Delehaye took for his editions of 1909 and 1925, and although it concerns Theodore the recruit it bears similarities to accounts of the martyrdom of Theodore the General that were current by the tenth century and a number of features that place it with little doubt in that time, whatever the date of any earlier material that it incorporates. Variants are extant, but of the *passio* alone, without the collection of miracles that follows and that is found in the Vienna codex.[65] That it was intended, like most such compositions, to be read out and listened to is evident from the author's opening remarks about the annual gathering to commemorate the saint at Euchaïta, addressed to his 'brethren' (183.1–15; 22–23), as well as from his concluding remarks leading into the miracle tales themselves (194.2–8).

Text 4 includes the episode of Theodore's mother's death and his father's ingenuity in fashioning a feeding-bottle for the baby, along with their names, as well as commenting on the saint's education until the age of 6 years, and thus shares a number of features in common with Text 3 (the short *vita BHG* 1765) and the encomium of Nikephoros Ouranos, along with the information in Gregory of Nyssa's homily, although, unlike in *BHG* 1765, there is no mention of his teacher's name, nor of Theodore's spiritual adviser who dwelt near the military camp. A new element is introduced when Theodore, having left the camp secretly for a desolate spot outside Amasia, prays to God to relieve his thirst, upon which a freshwater spring appears which, the writer assures us, can still be seen 'today' (Delehaye 1909: 186.18–33). Theodore then liberates a nearby settlement – Euchaïta is implied but not explicitly named – from an infestation of snakes and other beasts, a story that certainly existed by the time Chrysippos was writing, as we have seen; and he also meets Eusebia, who has now become not just a pious woman but a person of senatorial rank related to the imperial

---

63 See Hengstenberg 1912/1913: 99 and n. 1.

64 Ed. Delehaye 1909: 183–193; 1925: 49–52; discussion at 17 [21] – [23].

65 See Delehaye 1909: 26–32. The eleventh- or twelfth-century manuscript that has not survived (unfortunately destroyed in a fire in 1904: Delehaye 1925a: 17 [20]) contained a series of texts concerning Theodore, including a parallel version of this text: cod. Taurinensis CXL, c.IV. 18 (formerly c.V.32).

household (187. 7–24) (a feature shared with the encomium of Nikephoros Ouranos), and who warns him of the fearful serpent that dwells in that place and kills all who approach. A long exchange between the two ensues, whereupon Theodore calls out the dragon and slays it. But in contrast to the version in Chrysippos and in particular to the earlier account in Text 2 (*BHG* 1761), both of which go into considerable detail, the story of Theodore's interrogation, destruction of the temple (of Artemis) and eventual execution and martyrdom is recounted quite briefly.

As we would expect, the account includes elements from the older, established tradition, but now two episodes in particular – the dragon and Eusebia – are firmly linked and greatly extended. This would appear to be an elaboration of the dragon story recounted in the metaphrastic version of the saint's life and martyrdom noted above (*BHG* 1763),[66] from which we learn that the dragon was ravaging the locality around 'a certain place, called Euchaïta', and that it was the pious Eusebia, described as 'a woman from among the notables of the region',[67] who warned Theodore of the dangers of the monster.[68] This is the form Theodore's encounter with the serpent takes also in some accounts of the martyrdom of Theodore *stratēlatēs* (e.g. *BHG* 1751, but contrast with *BHG* 1752 – Text 5 below – which has neither serpent nor Eusebia, a trait common also to the Coptic and Armenian versions of the General's martyrdom)[69] current by the later ninth century, as indicated by the encomium penned by Niketas Paphlagon, mentioned above.[70]

It is possible to trace, in broad outline, the evolution of the stories of the martyrdom of St Theodore across the several centuries from the fourth to the eleventh and twelfth. Three features in particular have generally been passed over, but they are in fact of considerable interest in this respect. First, as we have seen, opinion is divided as to whether or not the story of the serpent or dragon evolved out of an original tale (in which Theodore expelled vipers and evil spirits from the region of Euchaïta as he was being taken to his place of execution) into his fight with the beast after he had arrived at Amasia with his unit, and whether it was perhaps conflated or

---

66 Ed. Delehaye 1909: 136–150; 1925a: 39–45.

67 The text later notes that she inherited her estate through her family: ed. Delehaye 1909: 137. 29–138.1 (1925a: 40§3).

68 Ed. Delehaye 1909: 137. 4–26.

69 For the Armenian and Coptic versions see respectively Conybeare 1896: 220–237 and Winstedt 1910: 73–133.

70 See p. 8.

deliberately integrated at some point with earlier pagan cultic legends or practices associated with the area. While clearly a development of the fifth or more probably the sixth century, as its interpolation into Text 2 suggests, the dragon-slaying tale was in existence in some form by the seventh century at the latest, indicated by the archaeological and sigillographical evidence. But at some point this theme then became linked to the tale of Eusebia, originally merely the standard pious female who can be found in a number of such accounts of martyrdoms, who preserved the saint's remains, in some versions taking them then to her home in Euchaïta.

Secondly, it is significant that from this point Eusebia had her role expanded to become, in the tenth-century metaphrastic version, a local notable and, by the time Nikephoros Ouranos composed his encomium to Theodore, a senatorial member of the imperial family, who both warns Theodore of the peril he faces from the serpent and – as in the earlier versions – later takes his remains and inters them in a tomb near her home at Euchaïta, where she builds a chapel for the saint. This version of Eusebia, the noblewoman associated with the family of the emperors Maximian and Maximinus, is that found also in *BHG* 1764 (Text 4) and in John Mauropous' eulogy for her, pronounced on her feast-day, the Saturday of the mid-Lenten week.[71]

It would be misguided to give too much credence to any of the details of these martyrdom narratives. Yet, on occasion, it is likely that known events or historically grounded tales lurk behind some of the rhetoric of the texts. In this case, the details of Eusebia's lineage and her exile under imperial protection do bear a clear similarity with events associated with a number of imperial women in the fourth century, and it is possible that the hagiographer – depending on the date of composition of the original account – could have known of them from reading historical or chronicle sources available to him. Eusebia was not an uncommon name, of course: the second wife of the emperor Constantius II was called Eusebia,[72] although there is unlikely to be any connection here. In contrast, the sister of Maximianus (C. Galerius Valerius Maximianus – Caesar 293–305, Augustus 305–311)[73] was also the mother of Maximinus Daia (Augustus 309–313),[74] and although her name is unfortunately not known, both of her imperial relations were involved in the early fourth-century Christian

71 De Lagarde 1882: 202–207.
72 *PLRE* 1: 300–301.
73 *PLRE* 1: 574–575.
74 *PLRE* 1: 579–580.

persecution. Had she had been Christian she might well have been sent away to country estates in the context of the persecution. Other imperial women who may have been conflated with our Eusebia might also include Eutropia, the wife of Maximianus Herculius (Diocletian's colleague). Eutropia travelled with Constantine's mother Helena to the Holy Land in the 420s and, although neither Eutropia's husband nor her son were Christian, she is assumed to have converted after the death of her husband in 309/310.[75] The tradition of exiled or disgraced imperial women being active in religious affairs in the Holy Land in general over the course of the fourth and fifth centuries might well have been recognisable to a late Roman audience; indeed, the figure of Eusebia may well have been introduced or expanded upon in order to make a veiled request to Eudocia for support for a church more attractive and appealing. We cannot know. But more likely still is that the story of these women, known from earlier sources that were available to the learned middle Byzantine authors of hagiographical writings, may readily have been redeployed in creating an account of the pious Eusebia at a later date.

Such variations as those concerning Eusebia, along with others, reflect the different preferences and concerns of both composer or redactor and audience or readership. In some variants there is no mention of Euchaïta as Eusebia's home; in other accounts, as in the version in *BHG* 1764, reference is made to her considerable properties and to her estate at Euchaïta, and the story ends with her own death and the interring of her body close by that of the saint himself.[76] Eusebia herself, as Text 4 makes clear, eventually became honoured as a saint and the subject of a commemorative feast, mentioned also by John Mauropous.[77] But her transformation, from a simple pious woman into a member of an imperial family and an owner of a country estate, is probably a reflection of the tastes and interests of the member or members of the provincial élite around Euchaïta in the tenth and eleventh centuries who may have commissioned the encomium and 'life before the martyrdom' or who may have been locally important members of the congregation to whom the text may have been read out on the saint's feast-day.[78] In any case, the text has clearly been added to and altered, so

75 *PLRE* 1: 316; Lenski 2004: 116–117. Note also Sozomen, *Historia ecclesiastica* 9.2, who relates the story of the aristocrat Eusebia, who established a martyrium for relics of the forty martyrs on her estate near Constantinople, a building that later became part of the monastery established there when she died. See Bowes 2008: 111–112.

76 Delehaye 1909: 187.21–188.24; 193. 3–11.

77 Delehaye 1909: 193. 3–11; Mauropous: de Lagarde 1882: 202–207; *BHG* 632.

78 See pp. 6–8 above.

that it is difficult to claim that any single element can be used to locate it in a period earlier than the tenth century.

In the third place, a key feature of this version is the great deal of detail accorded to the dragon and Eusebia story compared with the very sketchy reference to the trial and martyrdom themselves. Such a shift in the balance of miracle accounts has been observed in a number of other examples from middle Byzantine hagiography.[79] In the earlier accounts the trial and passion are the key moments; indeed, as we have seen, the trial narratives in the earliest martyrdom stories were based on actual proceedings in Roman courts, although it is impossible to say whether this was also the case for Gregory of Nyssa's encomium (if that is indeed the first one). In Chrysippos' encomium as well as the earlier account of Gregory of Nyssa it is the trial and martyrdom that are centre-stage. In marked contrast, the later accounts push the trial into a minor place at the end of the story, with much more emphasis placed on the heroism of the saint in dealing with the dragon as well as on his gentlemanlike behaviour and piety in relation to Eusebia. Indeed, the account is of an altogether more chivalric–heroic quality than the earlier versions. This, again, marks the text out as a later composition, reflecting in particular the interests and values of the provincial élite of the empire as well as the cultural milieu of the composer or editor.[80]

The date of composition of Text 4 cannot be determined exactly, but that it is a product of the tenth or eleventh century seems certain. But one feature at least may hint at an earlier – perhaps originally seventh-century – stage in its evolution. In the final section of the martyrdom the author expresses a prayer to the saint to bring back those who had been scattered by enemy action and rescue those who had been captured by the Arabs (193. 12–25): 'gather together those who have been scattered and bring back those who have been carried off into captivity on account of our many transgressions by the accursed Hagarenes...'[81] and, while Hagarenes technically meant Arabs, it could be applied to any eastern Islamic enemy.[82] The date of the manuscript does not help here, since it is generally attributed to the mid–late eleventh or early twelfth century. The reference may be part of the original prayer associated with the collection, and thus straightforwardly indicate contemporary or near-contemporary events in the context of the more-or-less constant warfare with the Arabs in the second half of the seventh

79 White 2008.
80 See above, pp. 30–31; also Efthymiadis 2011b: 96–98; 115–130; and Cheynet 2003.
81 Delehaye 1909: 193. 20–22.
82 See Shahid 1984a; 1984b s.v. Hagar, Hagarene.

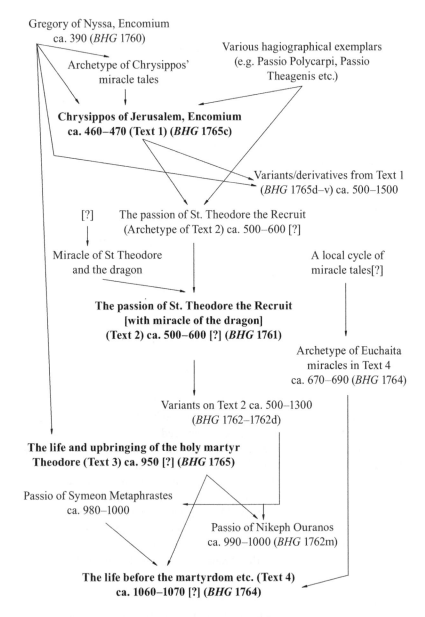

Gregory of Nyssa, Encomium
ca. 390 (*BHG* 1760)

Archetype of Chrysippos'
miracle tales

Various hagiographical exemplars
(e.g. Passio Polycarpi, Passio
Theagenis etc.)

**Chrysippos of Jerusalem, Encomium
ca. 460–470 (Text 1) (*BHG* 1765c)**

Variants/derivatives from Text 1
(*BHG* 1765d–v) ca. 500–1500

[?] The passion of St. Theodore the Recruit
(Archetype of Text 2) ca. 500–600 [?]

Miracle of St Theodore
and the dragon

A local cycle of
miracle tales[?]

**The passion of St. Theodore the Recruit
[with miracle of the dragon]
(Text 2) ca. 500–600 [?] (*BHG* 1761)**

Archetype of Euchaita
miracles in Text 4
ca. 670–690 (*BHG* 1764)

Variants on Text 2 ca. 500–1300
(*BHG* 1762–1762d)

**The life and upbringing of the holy martyr
Theodore (Text 3) ca. 950 [?] (*BHG* 1765)**

Passio of Symeon Metaphrastes
ca. 980–1000

Passio of Nikeph Ouranos
ca. 990–1000 (*BHG* 1762m)

**The life before the martyrdom etc. (Text 4)
ca. 1060–1070 [?] (*BHG* 1764)**

3   The possible textual evolution of
the Passio and Miracula S. Theodori tironis

century. But it would in any case not be necessary to emend it for it to evoke, for a mid-eleventh-century audience, more recent developments that directly affected the town and people of Euchaïta and its region: namely, the arrival of invading Türkmen nomads from the 1060s onwards. As noted in the Introduction, the area appears to have been overrun by the Turks shortly after 1071 and, if not a product of the eleventh-century redactor, written with these developments in mind, even an earlier text would still retain its immediacy and relevance for the period.

It remains to comment briefly on the other St Theodore, *stratēlatēs*, the General, who appears at some point in the ninth century. As noted above, this doubling of saints was not unique,[83] and, as we have also already seen, the first attestation of Theodore the General is the encomium to Theodore *stratēlatēs* composed by Niketas David Paphlagon in the late ninth or early tenth century (*BHG* 1753).[84] Possibly somewhat older than, or contemporary with, this there was also a martyrdom, purportedly the account of an eye-witness to the events, a certain Augarus (*BHG* 1750), upon which a number of variant versions were based.[85] The basic story, as found in the tradition that develops thereafter, concerns a well-born soldier of Christian parents, Theodore, a *stratēlatēs*, who comes to the attention of the emperor Licinius because of his wisdom and his bravery, especially in the slaying of a fierce dragon that infested Euchaïta. Theodore had been warned of the dragon by the pious Eusebia, and when he killed it many pagan soldiers who had seen the fight converted to Christianity. Licinius sends envoys to Theodore, who is in Pontic Herakleia, and requests that he come to him in Nicomedia; but Theodore, having treated the messengers with honour, sends his own letter to the emperor suggesting that he receive him in Herakleia and that he bring his gods with him. While the emperor travels with his army to Herakleia Theodore has a vision in which God exhorts him to have courage, because He is with him. Upon the emperor's arrival Theodore mounts his horse and meets him, at which the emperor asks him on which day he would like to sacrifice to the gods. Theodore asks the emperor to entrust the images of the gods to him for a while, a request to which Licinius accedes; but, as soon as he can, Theodore cuts the gold and silver statuary to pieces and distributes the fragments to

83 Cf. pp. 7–8 above.
84 Ed. Delehaye 1925a: 83–89. See Paschalides 1999.
85 The text is edited in Van Hooff 1883. Variants: *BHG* 1751: ed. Delehaye 1909: 151–167 (see 154.5–31); *BHG* 1752 (our Text 5): ed. Delehaye 1909: 168–182, a metaphrastic version of the martyrdom which adheres more closely to the 'Augarus' account. See Delehaye 1909: 32.

the poor. When the emperor discovers this he has Theodore punished, of course, and tortured in various ways, and then after the most horrific mutilations he is crucified. Theodore is left for dead on his cross, but at night an angel descends, heals his wounds and frees him. When some soldiers are sent to cast the body of the martyr into the sea they see him well and alive, and are instantly converted to Christianity. A proconsul is then sent with several hundred soldiers to find Theodore, but when they see the miracles he works they too accept Christianity. Another servant of the emperor, in some versions called Leander, attempts to kill Theodore, but is killed by the converted proconsul, who is in turn slain, this time by a Hun. The riot that then follows is calmed by Theodore, who is eventually caught and decapitated on Licinius' orders. Theodore's remains are taken to Euchaïna[86] (or in some versions Euchaïta), to which streams of pilgrims go to see the saint's tomb and to be healed of a whole range of illnesses and diseases.

As with the martyrdom of Theodore the recruit there are several variations between the different versions – the episode with the dragon, for example, is not included in all manuscripts of the metaphrastic version, as in our Text 5 here (*BHG* 1752); Theodore comes from either Euchaïta or from Herakleia; the pious Eusebia is not always present; the names of the various characters – soldiers, officials and the like – vary; Theodore's letter to the emperor is on occasion set out at length; and so forth. That Licinius is the persecuting emperor is likewise unusual, since Diocletian or Maximian and Maximinus are more often the impious and evil rulers – an echo, perhaps, of Constantinian propaganda from the 320s.[87] The details of the torture and martyrdom are taken from the standard literature available to the author, including Eusebius' works. And while it was understood by some that Theodore the General was a separate saint, and that Euchaïna

---

86 On which see pp. 9–10 above.

87 Licinius was Augustus 308–324, see *PLRE* 1: 509 (Val. Licinianus Licinius). He was allied with Constantine in the civil wars and tolerated Christianity, supposedly issuing the edict of Milan of 313 jointly with Constantine, although announcements of toleration had been issued before this, by Constantine in 306 and Maxentius in 311, even if not observed widely, since neither was an Augustus and thus had only regional authority at best. See *ODB* 1: 676. Licinius defeated Maximinus in 313, and ruled as Augustus in the east. Licinius in fact appears to have been a neutral supporter of Christianity, and it was propaganda after his defeat in the civil war of 323–325 by Constantine I that blackened his name, especially in the writings of Eusebius of Caesarea. See Carrié and Rousselle 1999: 228–229. Whether he actually did persecute Christians after 316, as relations with Constantine deteriorated, remains unclear.

was the seat of his cult and had its own independent ecclesiastical establishment, it is not at all certain that, by the eleventh century at least, the separation of the two was clear to, or believed by, everyone – including John Mauropous, the archbishop of Euchaïta in the eleventh century, who seems to have regarded them as two aspects of a single heroic martyr.[88] Certainly by the later twelfth century several of the miracles worked by Theodore the Recruit in the earlier collections were ascribed by some writers to Theodore the General, while in his encomium of Theodore the Recruit Constantine Akropolites notes that there were three well-known Theodores: Theodore of Pergē in Pamphylia, Theodore the General and Theodore the Recruit.[89]

The miracles of St Theodore the General thus remain less well-documented than those of his subordinate, the Recruit. The tale of the slaying of the dragon appears in variants of the martyrdom, but other aspects of his wonder-working – his remains acted as a cure for illness and disease and as a source of salvation for those in the locality – are referred to in passing at the end of the martyrdom accounts, but without further elaboration.[90]

The miracle collections

As noted already, the two sets of miracles of Theodore the Recruit are quite unconnected and seem to have exercised no influence on one another, even though, as we have seen, in at least one manuscript (cod. Vind. theol. gr. 60) they appear together and are integrated to the extent that the details of the martyrdom in the Chrysippos version are largely omitted because they are given in the immediately preceding text.[91] The only features that connect them are the common traditions incorporated into the two versions of the life and martyrdom. But these prologues are essential elements of the whole, serving to legitimate and to authenticate the miracle stories by placing them in the context of the saint's original martyrdom and the source of his intercessory power. A standard element in all such texts is the constant reminder that the saint is merely the channel through which

88 See Delehaye 1909: 36–37; 1925: 23 (#47); de Lagarde 1882: 36.

89 Ed. Delehaye 1925a: 72–76, see 72 [2]. For Theodore of Pergē, martyred under Antoninus Pius: *BHG* 1747.

90 E.g. Delehaye 1909: 167.14; 182. 8–10; 1925a (Niketas David Paphlagon): 89. [13].

91 Discussion of the mss: Delehaye 1925a: 18–22, and see above, pp. 21–22.

divine power is expressed, a channel which is, however, part of the world of men and thus provides a less awesome and far more approachable source of divine authority.

The structure of Chrysippos of Jerusalem's encomium is straightforward: a prologue followed by the brief account of the life and martyrdom of the saint, followed by the twelve miracle tales, and concluding with a prayer addressed directly to St Theodore. The composition of the miracles which are included as part of the encomium to Theodore can be dated with reasonable certainty to the 460s or 470s, the period during which he was active at the church of the Resurrection in Jerusalem. That the miracles were quite soon thereafter in circulation as an independent collection, taking on additional features and appearing in different forms in different contexts, is clear from the occasional reference to them, or to a particular miracle story, in a range of writings stretching from the sixth century into the late Byzantine period.[92] Eustratius, the late sixth-century author of the *Life* of the patriarch Eutychius of Constantinople (552–565 and 577–582),[93] made reference to the encomium by Chrysippos and to miracles 6 and 7 in his treatise on souls;[94] and Theodore the Stoudite paraphrases six of the miracles in his own hymn to St Theodore.[95] As Sigalas showed, the tradition is continuous into the late Byzantine period, and while the details of the miracles changed in some respects, along with the selection of miracles used by different writers and redactors, the basic content remained remarkably constant.[96]

The Chrysippos collection was intended to be read out to an audience of monks, as the opening lines of the encomium make quite clear: 'My beloved fathers and brothers, I present to you in the present [encomium] the praise of a martyr, most illustrious among martyrs … ' (51.1–2). The text continues in the same style, with a marked emphasis on the speaker presenting and leading the praise and the listeners responding in the appropriate manner

92 The extant versions of the miracles are edited by Sigalas 1924: 310–339; another edition of the texts was published by Delehaye 1925a: 60–71; discussion on the dissemination of the miracles after Chrysippos is in Delehaye 1925a: 17–23 (with 17–18 on Chrysippos himself); Sigalas 1937: 94–99.

93 *PG* 86: 2273–2290. On Eustratius' Life of Eutychius see Cameron 1988; 1990.

94 See *ODB* 1: 754–755; Beck 1959: 410–411 with references; discussion in Sigalas 1921: 11–12; Delehaye 1925a: 19.

95 Pitra 1876: 361–365; Delehaye 1925a: 21 [36]. Theodore draws on miracles 1, 2, 3, 6, 11 and 12.

96 Sigalas 1921: 12–16; 1924: 295–309, with a detailed comparison of the texts at 310–339; and 1937: 94–99 with corrections and further discussion.

to his text (e.g. 64.4: 'Hear now ... '; 65.9: 'Next you will hear ...' ; 69.4–5: '... what I will tell you... '; 72.15: 'Come then, and listen ... '; 73.10: 'Listen now ... '). The final prayer (77.9–79.8), addressed directly to the martyr himself, reinforces the oral aspect of the encomium. As Sigalas noted in his edition, this form of address occurs frequently enough in the hagiological literature and certainly indicated the oral character of the material, at least in its original form. Somewhat later this aspect develops into a standard element, regardless of whether or not the text in question was to be read out loud to an audience or congregation.[97]

Since there was at the time of its original composition and delivery no church of St Theodore in Jerusalem it is likely that the encomium was delivered on the saint's feast day, 7 February, either in the church of the Anastasis in the same city, where Chrysippos held his positions, or in a monastic setting. The only clear reference to a date occurs in the twelfth miracle story, which makes reference to the fire – probably that of 465 – that destroyed the first church of St Theodore in Constantinople (built in the year 412), but in the course of which the house of the consul Sphoracius was saved. In gratitude, he then built a more magnificent church dedicated to Theodore.[98] Later versions of the story include the patrician's name, which is absent from the original account, but occurs in various forms, including both Sparakios and – perhaps more obviously, from the hand of a middle Byzantine redactor – Staurakios.[99] Apart from this reference to the city of Constantinople, the miracle stories themselves are apparently set in the city of Theodore itself, Euchaïta. The only oblique indication of Jerusalem or its environs as the place in which the encomium was delivered occurs in the first story, when the kidnapped boy, having travelled 'from people to people' with the man who 'borrowed' him, soon arrives among the Ishmaelites,[100] suggesting the familiarity of the listeners with this part of the world, one of the few geographically identifiable regions mentioned in the collection, and somewhat closer to Jerusalem than Euchaïta (60.9–10).

---

97 Sigalas 1921: 80; Efthymiadis and Kalogeras 2014: 249.

98 Sp(h)oracius was *comes domesticorum peditum* in 450–451, and was consul in 452: see *PLRE* 2: 1026–1027 (Flavius Sporacius 3). On the fire, see Schneider 1941: 383–384; Mango 1986a: 125, 127; and below, pp. 80–81.

99 See Sigalas 1924: 337.10 and apparatus.

100 On the origins of the term and the location of the Ishmaelites: Knauf 1992: 3, 513–520; Ishmaelite was a standard designation for 'Arabs' by this time: see Shahid 1984a; 1989: 154–159, 179–180. White 2013: 28, perhaps inadvertently, assumes that Muslims are meant here – hardly likely in a story written down some 150 years before Islam emerged.

Perhaps more relevant still, according to Chrysippos, the kidnapped boy was, at the time of the delivery of the encomium, an old man and also a priest (62.8–13) in the city where the encomium was pronounced, although whether in the church of the Anastasis is never stated.

The miracle tales focus almost exclusively on the saint's church in Euchaïta. The only exception is in miracle 12, concerning Constantinople. Even miracle 11, which is not really a miracle but a brief account of how the saint works his wonders, has the church of St Theodore as its key locus. Of the eleven accounts ostensibly set in Euchaïta, the church figures in all of them, while the annual commemoration and feast of St Theodore is mentioned in three (nos 1, 7 and 10). Offerings to the saint and his church play a significant role also, in miracles 2, 4, 6, 7 and 10. As with other such collections, the intention was, of course, both to reinforce the cult of the saint and to encourage faith in the martyr's wonder-working powers and the benefits of devotion to his cause.[101] Of the individuals who populate the stories, there are several references to the clergy of the church of St Theodore as well as to the laypeople who assist them, such as the watchmen or gatekeepers and their supervisor (see miracles 2, 4, 8 and 9). Other characters who appear include soldiers (miracles 2 and 9), the poor (miracles 2 and 5), children (miracles 1 and 6), a gang of thieves (miracle 8), unnamed benefactors, some of them wealthy, some poor (miracles 1, 2, 4, 7, 10 and 12), silversmiths (miracle 3) and fraudsters/thieves (miracles 1, 3, 4, 7 and 8, although thief-like behaviour is punished or tolerated in other miracles, such as miracle 5).

A particular motif in this collection is the saint's understanding, even sympathy with, certain forms of wrongdoing. Thus in miracle 5 the thief steals light-fittings from the church of the saint because of his poverty, but then repays the church handsomely; in miracle 2 the saint rewards the soldier who stole a hen, but who later repented, with the return of a horse; in miracle 3 the thief is punished simply by being revealed and compelled to return what was stolen; in miracle 8 the gang of thieves lose their sight, but no further punishment for their theft is inflicted; indeed, the saint orders that they be provided with food to see them on their way; and so on. Particularly touching is his understanding for the boy who wishes to take the bejewelled sword donated to the church (miracle 6). The saint is presented as being both a harsh judge of misdeeds and at the same time a sympathetic and sensitive witness to the human condition, judging each

---

101 See Efthymiadis et al. 2011.

case with Solomonic wisdom. Given that children, in this case boys (albeit of indeterminate age, but old enough to work as a shepherd or to covet a sword), are the focus of two of the twelve miracles (1 and 6), one wonders whether his concern for young people was also an aspect of his local cult. Another obvious element is the power of the saint to return or redeem what is lost – a child, a horse, a hen, jewellery or money – and the selection of these miracles in particular may indicate an intention on the part of the compiler (whether Chrysippos or an earlier compiler is not known) to identify the saint with a specific range of saintly attributes, in the same way that saints such as Artemius, Febronia or Therapon in Constantinople were associated with healing. This is a feature that appears in other miracle accounts, where the saint is praised for the mercy he shows in returning captives and prisoners to their homes, later variations on a motif evident from the first in miracle 1 of the Chrysippos collection.

In summary, the miracle stories included by Chrysippos in his encomium, or that he found in his exemplar, reflect the daily life of any late Roman town, with references to family, church-going, the annual festival to commemorate the martyrdom of the saint, local craftsmen, the presence – often threatening – of soldiers, social distinctions between rich and poor, the fear of social condemnation for perceived wrongdoing, the existence of the judicial system and the rule of law, respect for private property and, above all, the charitable activities of the local saint's cult and the piety of the ordinary believer.[102] Most of these themes are, as we might expect, also found in comparable collections. Among the miracles of St Menas of Egypt, for example, we find a series of very similar tales, including the chastisement but release of wrongdoers, the rescue of a child servant, the checking of fraud and deceit and so forth.[103] While the 'specialist' healing saints already mentioned – Artemius or Therapon, for example – dealt with physical ailments in particular (even if caused by spiritual impurity, as was generally understood), many collections of miracles and beneficial tales dealt with just the sort of material presented in Chrysippos' encomium of Theodore. And it was, as has been remarked, in the service of the saint, of his or her devotees, of their church and their commemoration that such

---

102 See Pratsch 2005: 225–289 for a taxonomy of miracles worked by middle Byzantine saints, a series of topoi that evolves out of the late Roman context within which the Chrysippos and other fifth-century collections developed. On the role and presence of the city or town in late antique hagiography and miracle collections, see now Saradi 2014.

103 For the Menas material: *BHG* 1250–1269m, with a recent translation of a late recension of five abbreviated miracle tales of Menas by Duffy and Bourbouhakis 2003.

collections functioned as both an inspiration and as a means of publicising the particular merits of a specific saint.[104] Part of the text of the chant sung during the evening liturgy on the feast-day of the saint (17 February) summarises Theodore's powers as follows:

> To all those who turn to you in faith, Theodore martyr, extend the God-given grace of your wonders, through which we praise you, saying: redeem prisoners, heal the sick, enrich the poor and keep safe those at sea; render the flight of servants vain and reveal what has been taken to those who were robbed, o athlete; teach soldiers not to steal; treat the requests of infants with sympathy; procure a zealous protector for those who fulfill your sacred commemoration ...[105]

These local concerns and interests were a standard feature of much late antique hagiographical writing.[106] The *Miracles* of Cosmas and Damian were set in Constantinople;[107] those of Cyrus and John in Alexandria;[108] those of Demetrius in Thessaloniki;[109] and those of Artemius and Therapon once more in Constantinople,[110] although occasional references to people from other towns or regions occur. Similar local concerns dominated the other comparable collections from the same or a slightly earlier period, and while there are exceptions (the collection of miracles of St Anastasius the Persian recounts events which occurred supposedly in both Asia Minor and Palestine, for example), the general picture is clear.[111]

We have seen that these were by no means the only miracle stories concerning St Theodore, many of which circulated independently or in different combinations. Chrysippos makes mention of the 'cures of all sorts of diseases that took place there [in Theodore's church at Euchaïta], the succour for all those in every sort of trouble, the visions by night and by day in which he always looks down in military gear ... '.[112] Some of the stories remained independent of collections of miracles of St Theodore but

---

104 See discussion in the Introduction above.

105 Text in Delehaye 1925a: 21; see *ibid.* 18.

106 For a discussion of these collections and the context in which they were generated, see Delehaye 1925b; Rydén 1993.

107 See the introduction to the edn in Rupprecht 1935; also Deubner 1907; and *BHG* 372–392.

108 Fernandez Marcos 1975 (*BHG* 477–479).

109 *Miracula S. Demetrii*, ed. Lemerle 1979: 45–241 (*BHG* 497ff.).

110 *Miracula S. Therapontis* in Deubner 1900 (*BHG* 1798); see Haldon 2007.

111 *Acta M. Anastasii Persae*, ed. Flusin 1992 (*BHG* 84).

112 Sigalas 1921: 59. 10–13.

appear in other mixed collections or isolated contexts: these include the miracle of the *kolyva* and various versions of the story of St Theodore and the dragon. They also include two different stories concerning images of the saint. In one case, an image of St Theodore in a church near Damascus was attacked by a Saracen, who was then miraculously punished for his crime. The tale was recounted by Anastasius of Sinai (*BHG* 1765s; *CPG* III, 7758 B[2]). The story of the miraculous image of the saint commissioned by the pious Eusebia is perhaps better known: here, the painter found he was unable to complete the commission until the saint appeared to him in soldier's garb. The story is attached to our Text 4 and to the encomium of Nikephoros Ouranos, and is extant in other versions also, as well as in an undated hymn of Constantinopolitan provenance.[113] Then there is the tale of how Theodore defended Euchaïta against a Gothic ('Scythian') attack in the later fourth century. The story of St Theodore the General appearing on a white charger at the head of the imperial cavalry at the battle of Dorostolon in 971 is recorded in several histories.[114] And, of course, the stories changed in the retelling over the centuries: for example, the first miracle story in the Chrysippos collection, of the boy who was taken and sold to Arab herdsmen and miraculously returned by the saint to his father, has become, in the encomium of Constantine Akropolites, the story of a young soldier captured by the Arabs during the reign of Basil II (976–1025) and returned to his grieving mother.[115]

The second collection of miracles again forms part of a more extensive work.[116] The text as a whole, as redacted by its later editor and composer, falls clearly into two major sections: the opening address praising the saint and his intercessory powers, followed by the life and martyrdom, discussed above; and the eight miracles with – as a coda to both the eighth (numbered miracle 10 in the manuscript) and the prologue with the martyrdom and prayer – the final laudatory comment on the saint's powers of intercession, and the doxology. Again, in structural terms as well there are similarities with other seventh-century collections, not only the miracles of St Demetrius. Both the latter and the text of the Theodore miracles are punctuated by short discursive or polemical passages (noted

113 See Maas 1912 for the kontakion.

114 In Leo the Deacon, John Skylitzes and in Zonaras (who mistakes Euchaïna – Theodoroupolis – in Anatolia for a similarly renamed fortress on the Danube): detailed discussion in Oikonomidès 1986.

115 Delehaye 1925a: 73–75.

116 Delehaye 1909: 1194–201; 1925a: 52–55.

above: 197.30–198.8, 199.6–19)[117] designed to strengthen the faith of the audience in the saint and to encourage them to have resolve, to persevere in the defence of their city, even if the danger so graphically described might now be over. This is quite standard: by way of comparison, the late seventh-century collection of the miracles of St Artemius likewise contains such passages, although in this case addressed to those who doubt the saint's miraculous intercession on behalf of the afflicted and the reality and efficacy of his miracles.[118]

This short collection is of considerable importance for the history of the Byzantine provincial world in the seventh century not only for the detail it offers about life in a provincial town during a period of warfare and invasion but also because it is one of the very few accounts written from a local perspective about a provincial city at all. Apart from the collections of the miracles of St Demetrius in Thessaloniki, all our other sources from the later seventh century are written from a Constantinopolitan perspective. Theodore's miracles tell us about the physical appearance of the city, about the reaction of its populace to attack and the devastation wrought by the invaders, about the role of the cult of St Theodore and about the nature of popular piety in the provinces. They present, in short, a graphic illustration of life for some of the inhabitants of a seventh-century Byzantine province.

The miracles attached to the later version of Theodore's biography may not represent an original complete collection since, in the enumeration in the Vienna manuscript, miracles 5 and 8 are absent. Zuckerman has plausibly suggested that in fact the two digressions that occur between miracles 4 and 6 and between 7 and 9 were at one point given numbers as though they were themselves miracle stories, a mistake that was then corrected by a later copyist without then adjusting the remaining numbers accordingly.[119] Whether this was really a mistake remains an open question – after all, 'miracle' 11 in the Chrysippos collection is not in fact a miracle but rather a reference to the efficacy of devotion to St Theodore in achieving the punishment of thieves and the return of runaway servants, but in the ms tradition is given a number as though it were, and it circulated separately or in other collections as a miracle.[120] Perhaps the later redactor found the attribution of numbers to passages

117 See Lemerle 1981, 2: 36–40.

118 For discussion of the structure of such miracle collections, see Efthymiadis 2014b; further discussion of the *Miracula S. Artemii* in Haldon 1997b.

119 Zuckerman 1988: 196, n. 19.

120 Delehaye 1925a: 23.

that were not actual miracle tales objectionable and removed the numbers, but failed to renumber the remaining stories. We cannot know, although Zuckerman's suggestion is the simplest and perhaps the most likely. In any case the collection appears to have had a relatively limited circulation – only one manuscript (cod. Vindob. Theol. gr. 60) of the text is extant, although, as we have seen, a version did exist in the Turin manuscript C.IV.18, destroyed in a fire in 1904.

As to the time when they were originally composed, scholars have proposed three different dates based chiefly on the opening lines of miracle 4: 'In the fourteenth year of the God-guarded and Christ-loving reign of Constantine, when the peace between Romans and Saracens was over, at the beginning of the seventh indiction ... .'[121] Abrahamse argued for an eleventh-century redaction but using earlier material, the position that is also accepted here; Trombley suggested that the miracles were written down soon after 663–664. In contrast, Zuckerman argued that it was compiled in the early 750s – in fact, shortly after 754 – which is the only year where a seventh indiction and a fourteenth regnal year coincide. This also coincided with the synod of Hiereia in 754, and the text thus conceals an iconodule agenda. This date was also argued by Kazhdan.[122] In contrast, Trombley noted that the year 754 was not in fact the fourteenth regnal year of Constantine V but rather his thirty-fourth, as he became co-emperor in 720 – this was the standard method of dating reigns and is confirmed by the numismatic evidence, including a rare bronze issue minted in Constantine's thirtieth regnal year, 749/50,[123] while he was also co-emperor with Leo IV from 751 onward. The eighth-century date has now been persuasively challenged by Artun, who reaffirmed the mid-660s as the time of composition, or at least the time of the last set of events described. Along with a series of additional arguments he demonstrated, first, that there is no iconophile agenda to be read out of the miracles and that the text cannot be read as an iconophile polemic;[124] second, that the

121 Delehaye 1909: 196. 17–18: Τῷ τεσσαρεσκαιδεκάτῳ ἔτει τῆς θεοφυλάκτου καὶ φιλοχρίστου βασιλείας Κωνσταντίνου, τῆς μεταξὺ Ῥωμαίων καὶ Σαρακηνῶν περαιωθείσης εἰρήνης, ἐν ἀρχῇ τῆς ἑβδόμης ἰνδικτιῶνος ....

122 Abrahamse 1967: 347–354; Trombley 1985; 1989; Zuckerman 1988 (followed by Walter 1999: 167–168); Kazhdan 1988. Delehaye 1925a: 17 had argued for a mid-tenth-century date, taking the emperor in question as Constantine VII and emending the text accordingly.

123 Trombley 1989: 5.

124 Artun 2008: 2–6. Additionally we may note that the nature and degree of iconoclast oppression has been substantially revised and may no longer offer the sort of context preferred by Zuckerman: see Brubaker and Haldon 2011.

historical context clearly cannot be forced to fit the 750s;[125] and, third, that whereas in the early 660s a treaty – agreed in 659 – had recently ended between Romans and Saracens, no such treaty existed in the early 750s, nor indeed was the success of recent Byzantine offensives on the eastern front likely to have promoted such an agreement.[126]

Both Trombley and Artun have pointed out that neither the Byzantine nor the Arabic and Syriac sources make mention of any wintering raids for the period ca. 743–755, in part because of the civil war during the reign of Marwan and the Abbasid revolution.[127] At the same time Constantine V campaigned against Theodosiopolis (Erzerum) in 754, and was therefore relatively close to any invading force which threatened his lines of communication, which an Arab attack towards Euchaïta would certainly have done.[128] In contrast, during the period ca. 663–678 wintering raids were an annual event;[129] although they continued thereafter, they were far less frequent and in the period 720 and afterwards very few are registered in the sources.[130] Miracle 4 records that the wintering raid against Euchaïta took place in the seventh indiction and after the breach of a treaty: 663/64 is the seventh year of an indictional cycle, and in about 663 Mu'awiya broke the peace treaty which had been agreed between the two powers in 659.[131] In addition, the Arab sources record a major wintering raid against Koloneia in 664 and, while it is not clear which Koloneia is meant – the Pontic or Cappadocian – if it was Pontic Koloneia it would bring Arab forces close to Euchaïta at just this time.[132] While the reference to a fourteenth regnal year of the emperor Constantine remains problematic, it is, as Artun showed, problematic for each of these explanations, and all the evidence apart from this fits with a date of 663/64.[133]

In fact, and bearing in mind the fact that the miracles themselves reflect a seventh-century situation, it seems much more likely that the later copyist or redactor simply miscopied or misunderstood this dating formula. As we have already seen, its content suggests strongly that the introductory *Vita*

---

125 Artun 2008: 6–8.
126 See Artun 2008: 9–10 and Kaplony 1996: 40–41.
127 Haldon and Kennedy 1980: 113.
128 Lilie 1976:164ff.
129 Lilie 1976: 69–88; see also Abrahamse 1967: 347–354.
130 Lilie 1976: 95f.
131 Lilie 1976: 68–69.
132 Lilie 1976: 69.
133 The seventh-century date now seems generally accepted: see, for example, Efthymiadis 2014b: 115, n. 37; although White 2013: 28–29 continues to follow Zuckerman 1988.

et passio is a later compilation, including elements (notably the elaborate and extended story of the saint's meeting with the senatorial Eusebia of imperial connections) that had developed by the ninth or tenth century and not earlier. This is also suggested by the fact that the first of the miracles, recounting the story of Eusebia and the image of Theodore, seems most likely to be a later addition to what was originally a coherent set of early miracles written by someone familiar with seventh-century Euchaïta and its environs.[134] In this tale the pious woman Eusebia, who had commissioned a portrait of Theodore, found that the artist to whom she had given the task was unable to complete it. But then Theodore himself appeared for the painter and enabled him to complete the image to Eusebia's satisfaction. The picture was, according to the hagiographer, 'preserved by the grace of God to this day'.[135]

As others have remarked, the idea that saints were concerned with the form and appearance of their depictions is a particular characteristic of tenth- and eleventh-century hagiography, although it may have evolved before this time.[136] Given the probably later date of the introductory *Passio*, or at least of the redaction that is extant in *BHG* 1764, it is likely that miracle 1 was incorporated at the time the collection was assembled, with this miracle added as a preliminary indication of the saint's miraculous power. *BHG* 1764 thus represents a probably eleventh-century compilation consisting of a tenth- or eleventh-century version of Theodore's martyrdom, with the addition then of a much older collection of material derived from a strongly local tradition from Euchaïta itself. This collection can reasonably be placed in the later years of the seventh century, when annual Arab raids and the devastation that accompanied them were still a feature of daily life. No later events are described, whereas all the stories relate to attacks on the city between the time of the Persian wars and the height of the Arab raiding into Asia Minor in the 660s and the decade following.

In this respect, therefore, this short collection bears some comparison with other collections of miracles of the period that deal with events associated with a particular saint and the city he or she protects. As has been pointed out, there are particular parallels with the miracles of St Demetrius of Thessaloniki, which also deal very specifically with a series

---

134   This was also suggested in passing by Artun 2008: 5.

135   Delehaye 1909: 194. 24–25.

136   See, for example, Mango 1972: 210–214 for texts relating to saints Theodora of Thessaloniki, Mary the Younger, St Nikon Metanoeite and Athanasius of Athos; Dagron 1978: 147–149; comments also in Zuckerman 1988: 202; Artun 2008: 5.

of attacks on the city and with the role of the saint in protecting the town and its inhabitants from the enemy that encircled it.[137] The Demetrius tales fall into two groups. The first, written by an otherwise unknown John, archbishop of the city at some point between 603 and 649, comprises fifteen miracles relating to events of the reigns of Maurice, Phokas and Heraclius. They were composed most probably at some point during the early part of the reign of Heraclius.[138] A second, anonymous, group of six miracles was written down some considerable time later, probably in the 680s, although it includes events from much earlier in the century as well as of its own time.[139] The first collection falls readily into two sections, with seven miracles at the beginning worked (mostly) to help individuals, followed by fifteen worked by St Demetrius on behalf of the city and in the context of a series of historically determinate events – sieges and hostile attacks – to which the audience or reader can make reference. All six miracles in the second collection except the last one (concerning the rescue of the bishop Kyprianos of Byzacena from captivity), which appears to be an addition to the original group, relate to similar city-wide events.[140]

The character of the second set of Theodore miracles is thus very different from that of the first collection, in the form transmitted in the encomium to St Theodore by Chrysippos. Whereas the latter are concerned with everyday life in a peaceful late Roman city, with the concerns, problems and sufferings of a range of ordinary townspeople at their centre, and – apart from reference to some specific events in Constantinople in the 450s in miracle 12 – with no very clear idea of the time across which the stories were supposed to have taken place, the seventh-century collection is almost entirely taken up with a relatively specific and quite short period of time in the history of Euchaïta, and with a clear indication of the time at

137 Zuckerman 1988: 196–197 noted that the story in miracle 4, about St Theodore defending the gate of the city against attack, is very similar to miracle 15 in the collection of miracles of Demetrios ascribed to the archbishop John. Walter 1999: 174, accepting the argument that the miracles in *BHG* 1764 date from shortly after 754, as argued by Zuckerman, suggests that this miracle of Theodore in *BHG* 1764 may therefore have been based on the Demetrios story. If, on the other hand, the decade of the 660s or somewhat later is the date of composition of the Theodore collection, such a dependency may appear less likely, indeed may even be reversed.

138 See Lemerle 1981, 2: 27–28, 32–34, 40–44, 79–81. Lemerle offers a detailed historical and critical analysis of the texts. The similarity has also been noted by Efthymiadis 2014b: 115.

139 Lemerle 1981, 2: 172–174.

140 Lemerle 1981, 2: 162–163.

which the stories were written down. In miracle 4 the writer refers to the older and clearly well-known story about how in olden days the saint saved the city from 'the fierce Scyths and Huns' (i.e. the Goths), events that in fact occurred in 378 or 379; and in miracle 2 he refers to more recent but still long-past days, when the Persians had attacked Euchaïta (197. 2–3; 194. 28).[141] The earliest Persian attack on the city cannot have been much before 611, while the last Saracen raid mentioned, in the seventh and eighth miracles (nos 9 and 10 in the ms), and described as 'the yearly raid', is most probably one of those that took place before 678. The indictional and regnal years given in miracle 4 are specific enough to suggest, perhaps, reference to a written record, and a fairly recent time. The sense of temporal immediacy is underscored by the fact that the city of St Theodore is at the very heart of the tales in a way that the audience appears to have been expected to remember and recognise: Euchaïta and the area around it, including a number of quite specific references to particular locally understood landmarks, is the focus. While the Persian raids are described as having happened 'long ago', the attacks of the Hagarenes are clearly events within recent memory for those to whom the miracle stories are addressed. The composition of our miracle collection, therefore, is likely to have been within a few years of these events, at any rate before the end of the seventh century.

There seems little doubt that the author of this collection of tales was a local man, most probably someone closely associated with the church of St Theodore and perhaps with the local episcopacy – perhaps even a bishop himself. The description and casual mention of various aspects of the town and its environs (in the miracles numbered 7, 9 and 10), of the nearby mountain known as Omphalimon, of the Lykos river and of the chapel erected in the saint's honour after a Roman victory over the invading Persian forces (miracle 3) suggest as much, as does reference to the bishop Eleutherios in miracle 2, mentioned as though his name were familiar to the audience, which may also hint that the writer of the collection was associated with the local church administration – again a similarity with both collections of the miracles of St Demetrius. In either case the character of the collection, almost completely taken up with hostile attacks on Euchaïta and its survival thanks to the intervention and care of St Theodore, is very similar to that of the collections of Demetrius miracles,

141 For the Goths and the threat to Euchaïta in the later fourth century: Zuckerman 1991: 481–486.

and with them forms a unique testament to the conditions of the times and the daily struggle for survival against an unremitting and merciless foe.

Unlike the Chrysippos collection, or even the opening sections of the first collection of Miracles of St Demetrius, this group of St Theodore's miracles includes no reference at all to the healing of the sick or the resolution of personal calamities such as theft. What, therefore, might have been the context for this particular assemblage? Had the collection been composed with a general homiletic intention, in which the general concerns of ordinary people were addressed and illustrated by reference to the sort of day-to-day issues presented in the miracles incorporated into the fifth-century encomium, we would surely expect more tales dealing with such issues. Yet they are entirely absent. Instead, we have seven stories concerned entirely with warfare and the danger presented by invaders, and situated across a relatively short period of time. Each of the stories features incidents that occurred in moments of extreme crisis for the town and its populace and might well have been readily recalled by many, perhaps even recorded in some form, thus providing a source or sources for the redactor of the tales.

Two possibilities suggest themselves. First, the collection might reflect a deliberate attempt towards the end of the seventh century to produce a text that would directly address the anxieties and concerns of a congregation faced by the reappearance of the enemies described in the miracles. The reference to the Hagarenes and the prayer to Theodore to return captives taken as prisoners would add support to this possibility. One good reason for this may have been to try to dissuade the population from abandoning their town, as was apparently almost the case after one raid, described in miracle 7, and prevented by the saint's intercession with God (198. 28–32). The east Roman church was especially concerned with the abandonment by the clergy of their provincial flocks at this time, so again the collection may well reflect these sorts of concerns and an effort to address them by deploying and invoking the ideological weapon of saintly protection.[142]

Alternatively, the selection of these tales to the exclusion of others with different, non-military themes may be the work of the (or a) later redactor, perhaps in response to a similar threat in his own time. There are not many possible contexts after the middle of the eighth century. We

---

142 Official concern about the impact of warfare on the provincial clergy and their congregations, as well as on church property, is reflected in the canons of the Quinisext council of 691–692: see, e.g. Rhalles and Potles 1852–1859, II: 344 (canon 18); see Haldon 1997a: 128–129.

have already excluded the middle years of the eighth century – few if any Arab raids appear to have reached this part of Anatolia after the 740s. The major attack launched under Ma'mun in 838 may have been seen as one such threat, however.[143] Thereafter we have to wait for the eleventh century, where the obvious context for such a situation would be the arrival of Türkmen raiders in this region of Anatolia from the 1050s.[144] In any case, it seems reasonably clear that the miracles at least belong to a seventh-century text, either in its original form or suitably revised, rather than a new composition of our later, perhaps eleventh-century, redactor. The inclusion of the miracle of the saint's picture is the only tale that does not fit this profile, but its presence in the collection reinforces the suggestion that what we have here is in effect a prologue and *passio* redacted in the eleventh century, probably based on a much earlier exemplar, a collection of seventh-century miracle stories, and the insertion into this collection of the story of the icon, perhaps intended as a somewhat crude link between the two parts of the text.

The collection is quite brief, but we have already seen that there were other stories about Theodore in circulation, perhaps many of them known to the audience. In the introductory prologue the author notes that he will recount only the greatest of the miracles, since there is no time to include all that he had heard (194.3–8) – perhaps his audience is aware of those miracles deriving ultimately from the Chrysippos text discussed above, as well as others, circulating independently or with Chrysippos' original encomium. As with the miracles of St Demetrius, the author of the original collection of Theodore miracles also spoke to his congregation or listeners directly, as the inclusion of two homiletic sections at 197.30–198.8 and 199.6–19 and as his address to them as *philochristoi*, 'Christ-loving' or as *agapētoi*, 'beloved' might suggest. Neither this, nor the fact that the later redactor addresses his listeners as *adelphoi* (183.22), precludes the likelihood that the original text was probably intended for a broader congregation of townspeople as much as for a monastic audience.

---

143 On which see Auzépy 2008: 256; Kaegi 2008: 391–392.

144 The first Turkish attacks were into Armenia and the easternmost regions of Anatolia in the mid-1040s, but by the mid-1050s they were raiding much deeper into the region. By 1059 they were dangerously close to cities such as Euchaïta – in that year Sebasteia was sacked by the raiders after the Armenian garrison abandoned its defence (Matthew of Edessa, 111–3/117 [and cf. 166–7]).

3

TRANSLATIONS

Note: quotations and citations from the Septuagint follow L. Brenton, *The Septuagint version of the Old Testament and Apocrypha, with an English translation and with various readings and critical notes* (London–New York 1900/Grand Rapids 1972); quotations and citations from the New Testament are from the *English Standard Version*.

***

Text 1: *BHG* 1765c, ed. Sigalas 1921: 50–79; Delehaye 1925a: 55–72[1]

[50] *Encomium of Chrysippos, priest of Jerusalem, on the holy martyr Theodore, together with a partial account of his miracles*[2]
[51] As I present to you at this time the eulogy of this most illustrious among martyrs, my beloved fathers and brothers,[3] I ask that you all share jointly in this earnest endeavour, firstly strengthening it through your prayers and secondly, after this, through your zeal in listening. For while I will utter the words, you will appreciate their value through deeds; I will provide the voice, you will supply the ears; I will set the lyre in motion, you will effect the strokes; I will move the strings, you will provide the harmony of the audience. Let us share this zeal with one another at the present time, since in my undertaking of this laudation certain of you, as you know, stirred me to it, without my previously considering it, promising that my reward for the effort put into the text would be the delight in the words themselves

---

1 Page numbers in the body of the text are to the Sigalas edition.

2 For the trial and martyrdom Chrysippos follows the details provided in the homily on Theodore by Gregory of Nyssa, changing some and rearranging others of the episodes.

3 See Sigalas 1921: 79–80 (to 51.2); 1937: 83 on 'beloved fathers and brothers', who takes it as a clear indication of a monastic audience. As Efthymiadis and Kalogeras 2014: 249 note, however, this is not necessarily always the case and should probably not be taken for granted. Further on hagiographical authors see Hinterberger 2014b.

through the action of the martyr. So, although I know that I can say nothing of worth on the subject, still I am confident that the gift to be presented to him who is praised is acceptable, since I also believe that at all events those who appealed to me did so in earnest and not without his approval for it.[4] Let the radiant martyr Theodore therefore be crowned in word by us also; let him be crowned by us, although until now we have no holy church for him here;[5] let him be crowned by us since the power of all the saints is everywhere present, and all those through whom they act are everywhere known. But what, what are the means by which I alone must weave the crown? Which are the first blooms that must be brought to him? For some are provided to us by the meadow of martyrdom, others by the meadow of his miracles. So which shall I present first? The events of his martyrdom display wonderful courage for the faith, while his miracles bring greater pleasure to the ear; the former claim a greater share in nobility of purpose, the latter in the workings of grace. And yet let the events that came first in time come first also in the story. So let us speak first about the martyrdom. [52] The emperors who ruled on earth at that time[6] waged a shameless war against the king of heaven, or rather not just of heaven but of all creation.[7] From below these impious men launched a bold campaign against the heavenly sphere, and from below clay took aim at its own maker and spread a teaching that compelled people to *serve the creature rather than the Creator* and to indulge gods that were no gods with honours from polluted sacrifices.[8] And then they set up altars everywhere, they lit defiling fires everywhere, everywhere they corrupted the earth with the stench of sacrifice and with blood, defiling the air, putting forth a stench vile to the angels, and provoking God, since he had been treated with ingratitude by his own creatures. It was at that time that the martyr was conscripted for military service[9] because of his physical nobility, although in his heart he

4 Sigalas 1937: 89 suggests that the declarations of his not being fitted to deliver such an encomium are evidence of this being Chrysippos's first such laudation.

5 The first mention of a church of St Theodore in Jerusalem is for the year 532, in the *Vita S. Sabae* 185. 5 (§78).

6 Chrysippos avoids referring to any of the characters in the encomium and in the miracles by name, with the exception of Theodore himself. See also Leemans 2006.

7 On the play on the opposition between the heavenly and the earthly king, see below [52.13–14; 56. 8–12]. For a sensible short analysis of the standard structure and content of the *Life and martyrdom* genre, see Detoraki 2014.

8 Rom. 1. 25; for polluted meat from sacrifice, see also 1 Cor. 8. 1–13; Acts 15. 20.

9 *Strateia/στρατεία* = Lat. *militia*. Technically military service, but the word referred from the reign of Diocletian to any form of state service, civil or military: see Jones 1964:

served a duty far better than that which was visible, namely that which was unseen.[10] And when he wished to reveal this he spoke out clearly to all, that he served the heavenly king, rather than the earthly rulers, naming with the Father also the Son and then the Holy Spirit. These things then became for him the grounds for his brilliant martyrdom, for the commander of the unit,[11] being the first to learn of his openness of speech[12] in such matters, undertook to interrogate him and to banter with him, and brought forward the following challenge against him, as though it were very wise: 'Does your god have a son then, just like a man?' The saint responded to this – the words were brief but full of life, 'Yes indeed, truly my God has a Son, a Son who is Himself God and the Word, a Son through whom He created everything.'[13]

Such was the first proving-ground, that of the courageous speech of the martyr. What deed then followed? What did he produce of even greater daring?

Seeing that the servants of the tyrannical dogma remained unsated by the injustice against those who wished to express their piety, but rather [53] assigned some to various sorts of torment, condemning others to death, he could not bear to remain quiet during such events, and so devised a deed worthy of the Lord and carried it out. For what did the Saviour say? '*I did one work and you all marvel.*'[14] So, therefore, he too confounded all the champions of the idol through one act, he astonished them all, he led them all to grief and inconsolable suffering. And what was this deed? He destroyed by fire the temple that they revered most of all, lighting the fire all by himself at night. And it was most revered not without reason, for it was dedicated to the mother of their so-called gods, so that a great deal more was burned, since along with the mother the whole collection of

---

377–378; and for its Byzantine value: Oikonomidès 1972: 283–287. This version of the *passio* by Chrysippos makes no mention of the martyr's age at this point.

10 In *BHG* 1761 (Text 2) this is the point at which the story of the dragon is inserted.

11 Given the name Bringas in Text 2.

12 *Parrhēsia* (παρρησία), openness or liberty of speech, carried a wide range of significations in a Christian and Biblical context: see Lampe 1961: 1044–1045 s.v. As an attribute of the OT prophets it was similarly applied to Christian saints and martyrs. In the hagiographic tradition, as in the texts translated here, it features prominently in the accounts of saintly intercession with God and in accounts of the relations between holy men and emperors. See Rapp 2005: 260–273; Detoraki 2014: 68.

13 Cf. the similar passage in the homily by Gregory of Nyssa (64.23–67.2; trans. Leemans 2003: 87).

14 John 7. 21.

demons was slighted in the act.[15] When then a wicked informer brought the issue before a yet more wicked magistrate, hurling many abuses at the martyr, before the magistrate had barely begun to ask questions,[16] the saint of his own accord confessed to the accusation quite openly, crying out, 'It is my doing, I do not deny the deed – rather I am exceptionally proud of it!' In addition to these words he also added his own insult to this idol, inquiring why, if such was the mother of their gods, she had been unable to rescue herself from the flames. The confusion among the impious could not be expressed in words, for the magistrate ordered the executioners to raise their hands against him and to smite his mouth, threatened to lacerate his cheeks and delivered him over to even bitterer torments. But this did not weary his greatness of spirit based on faith, neither did what he had suffered, nor what he was about to suffer. So straight away he was condemned to prison in chains and to the bitterest hunger, the magistrate having commanded that he was to be confined in such a way that food should not be brought to him from any source at all. Yet again he neither gave way nor surrendered to any of this.

Then there took place something very similar to the miracle that happened of old to Paul, yet even more marvellous. For when all Paul's chains were entirely shattered [54] by some mysterious power, he had as his fellow prisoner and cellmate Silas; upon which the gaoler, raising his sword against himself, gained by the sword salvation through baptism.[17] Very

15 See the comparable account in Gregory of Nyssa's homily (67.3–24; trans. Leemans 2003: 88), with brief discussion in Limberis 2011: 201–203. The cult of Cybele was well-established throughout western and northern Anatolia. See above, p. 24. One might ask whether this motif of the destruction of a temple owes anything to the story of the actual destruction by fire of the temple of Artemis at Ephesus in 356 BC, not long after its completion, in a vainglorious act of arson by a certain Herostratus: see Valerius Maximus, ed. Briscoe 1998: viii, 14. 5.

16 A key topos of the martyrdom genre was the betrayal of the martyr: cf. *Acta Polycarpi* 1. 2 (306). Since Roman law was largely concerned with property rights, a case against a Christian required an accuser, who could be any free private person as well as someone holding public office, and a governor willing to hear a case based on the charge. In fact, many governors refused to countenance such cases, and it was primarily in response to the issue of an imperial edict proscribing Christian worship, churches and so forth that persecutions were undertaken. See de Ste Croix 1963; more generally on the persecutions Moss 2013; Castelli 2004; Barnes 1968; Bowersock 2002.

17 See Acts 16. 24–33. The episode of Paul's escape from prison with Silas was a popular motif in martyrdom accounts, along with episodes from the life of Jesus, the martyrdom of St Stephen, or accounts of the arrests and trials of Paul: see discussion in Detoraki 2014: 65–66.

similar, yet still more wonderful, was the case of the martyr. For while he spent the night in chains, first of all the Lord appeared to him and spoke, exhorting him to take courage and look to sustenance that was incorruptible rather than corruptible. But then afterwards, what else happened? As the martyr sang psalms all alone, there sang out loud along with him the voices of many people.[18] This disturbed the guards and made them rush to the cell door to investigate what was going on within – for, indeed, seeing confirms what is heard. And they beheld a great crowd around him, an angelic host, since it was possible to judge the value of what was seen also from the brilliance of what the senses perceived. Yet when these things were reported to the ungodly man [the magistrate], blinded by the fog of his impiety, he went off to the prison with many guards and, placing them with the others of the watch all around, he went inside. Finding none other than the martyr, still bound, he experienced the same fear as the gaoler of old, but did not follow along the same road to salvation, nor did he fall down as did that other gaoler, neither did he ask, '*Lord, what must I do to be saved?*'[19] That impious fellow, rather, proceeding from darkness to darkness and persevering in his own original orders, conceded only so much, that he permitted one ounce of bread and a cup of water to be given to the martyr, through which he expected nothing less than that this would again bring about the martyr's death. Yet here again, in the superiority of his self-restraint, the martyr defeated the transgressor's design, not deigning even to taste any of the proffered food and drink, but saying that what had been given to him by Christ was sufficient.

Such was the second proving-ground for this invincible martyr. So, come now, come and learn the nature of the third stage of his trial.[20]

For this imitator of the dragon of the mind[21] made a pretence of adopting a kindly attitude, I suppose, counselling and advising what was expedient, [55] promising him the position of high priest[22] and other

18 In the homily of Gregory of Nyssa this story is placed after the interrogation and torture that followed the burning of the temple. See for this motif also Limberis 2011: 36.

19 Acts 16. 30. Cod. Paris gr. 1452 gives a little more detail of the story in Acts.

20 I.e. of the martyr's suffering before his martyrdom. Cf. V. Theod. Syk., §107. (and cf. Dawes and Baynes, *Vita Theod. Syk.*, comm. to §107, at 190).

21 I.e. the devil, in opposition to a physically real dragon (νοητός/*noētos* as opposed to αἰσθητός/*aisthētos*); cf. Sigalas 1921: 85, n. to 54.27. The dragon was commonly equated also with Satan, of course: see, e.g., Revelation 12. 7–9.

22 Although one might also read for ἀρχιερεύς (*archiereus*) 'bishop' here rather than high priest. I thank Alice-Mary Talbot for this suggestion.

illustrious honours from the emperors.[23] But the martyr, even before he
finished speaking about these matters, holding out before him the weapon
of the seal of Christ,[24] also said such words as these: 'Why, o impious man,
disregarding the authority you possess, do you shift to flattery that is more
painful to me than torture? For my shame in denying the calling of my Lord
is more painful to me than every sort of torment. You have swords at your
disposal – take my body, hack it to pieces, give it over, if you want, to the
flames, share it out among the maws of beasts.' Then a stake was erected
and the torturers were ordered to smite his ribs. Yet he paid absolutely
no attention to what was happening, as if the iron claws were working
on another body.[25] Indeed, he was overjoyed that he was deemed worthy
of imitating the Lord on the cross, and taking from David his words of
thanksgiving, he chanted, *'I will bless the Lord at all times.'*[26] After this
there took place a remarkable debate between the martyr, from the stake,
and the impious magistrate from his tribunal. For the latter, in rebuking
him, described the sufferings of the Redeemer, the insults on the cross,
the ignobility of death; whereas the former, like the great forefather of the
martyrs, Stephen, filled rather with the Holy Spirit, along with the streams
of blood also vied eagerly with the impious magistrate with streams of
words and, by these words, as he was reproached, Theodore became
magnified in honour, as he was blasphemed, the martyr became glorified;
and holding forth, he praised such good fortune as comes to humankind
through the abuses suffered by those upon the cross, calling the magistrate
in addition a son of the devil. For who, if he have this Father, who could not
recognise who gives kings their power, magistrates their office and who
gives to him [i.e. the magistrate] the authority he wields? Who, if he have
this same Father, would compel the worship of that which is created rather
than the creator, and instead of the true God call stones and wood their
gods? What more need be said? For, refusing to respond to the martyr's
bold speech, the impious magistrate demanded that he state briefly whether
he wished to be of the party of those worshipping these things [56] or of

23 The passage faithfully follows Gregory of Nyssa's homily. Leemans 2003: 108 n. 8
notes a similar passage in the *Life* of Theodotus of Ancyra (*BHG* 1782).

24 I.e. making the sign of the cross. Cf. Lampe 1961: 1356, s.v. σφραγίς B.

25 The hero's ability to endure the most horrible torture and pain and his or her patience
in the face of adversity are key elements, of course: see Detoraki 2014: 68–69. For discussion
of the torture and sado-erotic violence in the early martyrological tradition, see esp.
Frankfurter 2009; for broader background Brown 1981; Grig 2004.

26 Ps. 34. 1.

that of his most beloved Christ. But hearing this alone, and jumping for joy, the martyr said, 'Now I shall be granted what I have striven for. For I wish to be forever with my Christ, or rather, I have been with Him and I am with Him and I pray never to be separated from His kingdom.'

And so, through these trials, some in words and some in deeds, he completed the third stage and accepted thus the cruel sentences of the tyrant. For what were they, what indeed? 'Since Theodore did not obey the emperors,' he said (the emperors – which ones? Those of the earth and upon the earth and returning again to the earth, those who possess all transitory and ephemeral things), 'but believing in Jesus Christ who was crucified under Pontius Pilate, let him be delivered to death by burning at the stake.' Yet are not these things more brilliant than a crown glittering with many-faceted stones? And more precious than a royal diadem?[27]

Having been despatched with such adornments to the place where the sentence was to be carried out, a most wonderful sight was seen there, too. With a joyous countenance, not as though going to the pyre but rather as if going of his own accord to a bath-house, after removing his clothing and loosening his shoes, he offered his hands behind his back to those who pressed around him. He who was to persevere until death would normally have been nailed up, but he promised to do this of his own accord and showed the use of nails to be unnecessary.[28] He thus also became [57] the priest for his own sacrifice, through the prayers that he uttered. And he also achieved a further success. Just as the Saviour on the cross took the thief as his companion on the journey to paradise, so Theodore drew the companion of his military service along with him through preaching of fellowship upon the pyre and of the road leading up to heaven.[29] And so within a short time the words of the martyr were fulfilled in reality; for he who was summoned to be a martyr followed the martyr. Such was the fruit that the pyre brought to him.

Blessed are those who were deemed worthy to behold that burnt offering with pure eyes, most blessed again is she who came into possession of the remains of those holy bones, distributing money in plenty to the watchmen so that she could store these abundant riches as a treasure in

27 Cf. *Acta Polycarpi* 18. 2 (326). For 'the third stage' of the martyr's trials, see n. 20 above.

28 Cf. the *Acta Polycarpi* 13.2–3 (320).

29 In later versions one or more of his companions are named (in Text 2, *BHG* 1761, for example, as Cleonicus); and, like Eusebia, eventually merited their own martyrdom accounts: see Delehaye 1909: 40–43.

her own house.[30] She was pious in name and in purpose, worthy to be ranked with Mary, worthy to be counted with Salome and to be mentioned alongside Susannah[31] – they brought unguents to the life-giving tomb – the house itself was chosen by her as a tomb for the martyr, and the same gift was also assigned by her later as the place for the original church and atrium.[32] For in her stead this noble martyr came to be established as owner and protector of the whole place.[33] Through these things, the martyrs are honoured, but Christ, who accepts every martyr's sacrifice, is honoured especially, Christ, who is Himself a martyr among martyrs, is honoured, '*So everyone,*' he said, '*who acknowledges me before men, I also will acknowledge before my Father who is in heaven.*'[34]

[58] Such, then, were the trials that took place during the martyrdom; but now the discussion must change course, to make mention of the wonders that were worked. For this, this confirms most clearly that the death of saints is no death, but rather a transfer to a better life than here on earth. The wise David is a witness to this when he sings of them, '*Precious in the sight of the Lord is the death of his saints.*'[35] For how was death precious unless it shared in true life? But, since time would not permit me to mention everything concerning the subject at hand, nor would speech be adequate, I will at the present time relate such things as might suggest themselves as fitting and will make them known, through the active power of him whom we praise.

30 The pious woman, Eusebia: see above, pp. 34–39, and Sigalas 1921: 86–87 (on 57. 8–11). As noted above, Chrysippos avoids the use of names throughout his encomium.

31 See Mark 16. 1; Luke 8. 3. Mary (Magdalene), Susannah and Salome (see also Mark 15. 40) were followers of Christ, who accompanied him from Galilee to Jerusalem and were present at the crucifixion. Salome is not to be confused with Salome the daughter of Herodias (Mark 6. 14–29; Matt. 14. 1–12). On both, and on Jesus' other female followers, see Witherington 1984.

32 The text has *τῆς πρωτοτύπου παστάδος τε καὶ αὐλῆς. παστάς/pastas* had a rich variety of meanings in Christian literature, referring to any structure rendered spiritually magnificent through association with Christ or a saint as well as to a bridal chamber, to spiritual marriage to the soul of Christ, to the Virgin Mary, or to marriage itself: see Lampe 1961: 1046, s.v. The church at Euchaïta is described in extravagant terms in the homily on Theodore composed by Gregory of Nyssa (62.25ff.; trans. Leemans 2003: 85). See also Sigalas 1921: 87 (on 57.14–17); Delehaye 1933: 199.

33 A topos for martyrs in the context of their burial place: see Sigalas 1921: 87 (on 57.16–17).

34 Matt. 10.32.

35 Ps. 116. 15. Quoted by Gregory of Nyssa in his homily (64. 3; trans. Leemans 2003: 85).

Yet there is time briefly to mention something about the aforementioned holy atrium of the martyr, which all the people of the Pontus – I mean, that which was once inhospitable but is now friendly[36] – possessed as a common defence,[37] as a shared haven, because the martyr extended his hand to all those who come to him from all directions. For since it can claim in all probability the whole treasure of his blessed remains, it surpasses all glories in distinction, and in it was the first and greatest wonder, the expulsion of the evil spirits. For the estate used to be full of all kinds of demons, as Isaiah said: 'hedgehogs shall make their nests there and laughing satyrs [59] have their home in it.'[38] But since, in the course of the completion of his martyrdom, the noble man was brought there and spent one night in it (because the hour constrained those who escorted him to do so), this immediately sufficed to purify the estate and provided the occasion for it afterwards to receive the church. As a result, as soon as anyone distressed by an evil spirit approached the boundaries of this church, the demon departed immediately, fleeing in utmost haste; indeed, since the martyr drove them out with severe beatings through his prayers, the sight of the place from afar still reminds them of their own evil deeds.[39]

But who could also recount the cures of all sorts of diseases that took place there, the succour for all those in every sort of trouble, the visions by night and by day in which he always looks down in military garb?[40] For not even now does he disown the military dress, even though he is

36 Strabo, *Geography*, vii, 3. 6. The earlier Greek description of the Black Sea as 'unfriendly', Πόντος Ἄξεινος (*Pontos Axeinos*) derived ostensibly from its stormy nature, as Strabo notes, and is found in older writers such as Pindar; but behind this appears to lie an earlier Iranian (probably Scythian) term for 'dark' – *Akšáena*: see Danoff 1962: 952–954.

37 An oblique reference to the well-known episode of Theodore's warding off an attack by the 'Scyths' – i.e. Goths – in the period 378–379, referred to in Gregory of Nyssa's homily. See Leemans 2003: 82; Zuckerman 1991: 481–486. Churches were also seen as metaphors for a defence against barbarians and non-Christians, as was, for example, the church for the three martyrs Tarachus, Probus and Andronicus that the bishop of Mopsuestia, Auxentius, planned to build: *Passio S. Nicetae*, 214. 15–19.

38 A loose paraphrase of Isaiah 13. 22: καὶ ὀνοκένταυροι ἐκεῖ κατοικήσουσι, καὶ νοσσοποιήσουσιν ἐχῖνοι ἐν τοῖς οἴκοις αὐτῶν· 'and satyrs shall dwell there; and hedgehogs shall make their nests in their houses'. Whether this episode is at the origin of the story of Theodore's fight with the dragon, introduced perhaps in the sixth or seventh century, remains unclear. See above, pp. 4–5, 27–28.

39 It was a well-established topos that the relics of a saint could drive evil spirits away, and that the latter were able to recall the scene of their defeat. See Delehaye 1933: 145ff.

40 A reference, perhaps, to an image of the saint in his church at Euchaïta.

enrolled among those who inherit the kingdom of heaven. And who, who could enumerate the people who enter there continually, who return from there, who appreciate the rewards on account of which they prosper, and for whom also this verse from the psalms was fulfilled: '*All that are round about him shall bring gifts*'?[41]

Now I will present, one by one and in sufficient detail, an account of the wonders worked everywhere by the martyr, and just as I said, selecting according to the appropriateness of the tale.

[Miracle 1] Sigalas 1921: 59.21–62.16; Delehaye 1925a: 60 [10]–61 [11][42]

A man endowed with great faith in the martyr, whom he had made guardian [60] of all that he owned, and who always celebrated with great joy the annual commemoration of his great benefactor, together with honours and feasts for him to the best of his ability, fell one day into misfortune. Now this man had a son and a donkey, the former still a youngster, while the donkey served his needs. Someone asked to hire the donkey for a short journey, and having persuaded him in this, persuaded him also to send his son along with the ass as well, promising to return with both as quickly as possible. So, since he had succeeded in his request, he set off on his journey, and *went from nation to nation*, as the Psalmist has it.[43] But having continued his progress and arriving among the people of

---

41 Ps. 76. 11.

42 Sigalas edited several versions of these miracles, together with details of variants by Theodore of Stoudios, John Mauropous, John Pediasimos or in the Menaia and the Synaxaria, and gives full details along with an analysis of the manuscript tradition (1924: 296–308). These were also edited and published by Delehaye 1925a, although his edition is somewhat difficult to use since the variant readings are incorporated into the critical edition of each text. I have preferred Sigalas' clearer versions (note Sigalas 1937: 90), and give page references to the variants in the notes to each miracle below (Delehaye's variants, as just noted, are included in the main reference for each miracle). References to these editions are given at the beginning of each miracle account. There are several variants or references to this miracle: Sigalas 1924: 310–317; Delehaye 1925a: 60–61. The details vary, and some accounts involve either the boy's parents or the mother, the boy becoming a captive of the Ishmaelites on a raid to Euchaïta (clearly a version that dates from the seventh century or later), or the captors are named as Persians and the evil man described as a merchant. As noted in the Introduction, many variant versions of these miracles circulated. In Theodore of Stoudios's version the saint is mounted on a white horse and the boy is described as αἰχμάλωτος/aichmalōtos: that is to say, as a captive in war: Pitra 1876: 364.θ.

43 See Ps. 105. 13.

Ishmael, he imitated the evil deed of the brothers of Joseph, and straight away gave the boy to the Ishmaelites, while he continued on to another land.[44] And so the annual commemoration of the martyr came around, but the man was grieving because of what had happened to his son, and did not take care of arrangements for the festival, nor did [61] he do any of the things he usually did. And when the martyr demanded his due, he retorted with the bitter blow from the loss of his child, adding to this yet harsher words, saying that in vain had he relied upon the martyr's patronage and expected his aid, in vain had he assumed that the martyr would protect all his family.

After this another commemoration came around.[45] And the man did the same, and made the same response to the same accusations. But now, behold with me the martyr's wonder-working! The boy had been placed by his master among his own shepherds, and went off with them to pasture the flocks in the wilderness. Now the martyr appeared near to the boy when he was apart from the other shepherds with him, in the guise of a soldier with a pair of horses, mounted on one while the other was riderless, and he inquired of him who he might be and from what land. Learning from him the truth of what had happened, he urged him to return with him to his home, offering him his other horse, and not only offering this, but with his own hands lifting him up from the ground and setting him in the saddle. As they journeyed thus together, whenever the boy needed to eat, the martyr opened the pouch he carried and took from it some food, the nature of which the youth did not recognise, but through which he felt not a little revived. Riding along thus, they completed the long road to the boy's home in a few days. When he was announced to the father [62] lamenting for his son, the latter's mind was torn between joy and astonishment. He rushed out and welcomed his son and went back indoors with him, to prepare some hospitality for the man who had appeared. But when he went out a second time to the man who had arrived with the horses, he had disappeared. Everyone was at a loss. Yet, when the father realised whose work this was, he went straight away from there to the church of the martyr, recounting the whole affair and the whole

44 See Gen. 37. 25–28. For discussion of the Arab/Ishmaelite nomads who inhabited the arid pasturelands and desert regions of Syria–Palestine, see Shahid 1984b: 285–288; and in general on the Arabs in the late Roman period, Shahid 1984a and 1989.

45 The context requires this to be the annual commemoration, thus a year later, as correctly seen by Sigalas 1937: 92, note to 61.5 (*pace* Delehaye 1925a: 60 [11], who suggested one of the other yearly feast-days for the saint: 1925a: 24 [49], 27 [58]).

good deed. And that the story is not made up, we need look no further for proof,[46] for the boy who was so miraculously rescued is still alive, and instructs all about what befell him: he who was young is now greatly advanced in age; he who was once with country shepherds is now with spiritual shepherds; he who once guided flocks through the wilderness now guides the church alongside the Lord our Guide.[47]

I know well that both the marvellous tale and its happy outcome are pleasing to us. Come, therefore, let us add to these things something no less wondrous or joyful.

[Miracle 2] Sigalas 1921: 62.17–64.4; Delehaye 1925a: 61–62 [12][48]

A needy woman who honoured the Benefactor with gifts from her poverty dedicated to him a hen which she had raised as an offering. But a soldier, seizing the hen, stole it and carried it off.[49] So the woman, running up

46 On the proofs associated with the miracles of saints see below, pp. 79–81.

47 The final sentence indicates a near-contemporary event – whether an accurate reflection of something known to some of the audience or a rhetorical device cannot be known – and probably means that the person in question had by then become a bishop. The story also underlines the fact that these were events that took place in the locality of Jerusalem itself. But the Ishmaelites were readily transferred in time, of course, and became in some of the later versions the Arab Muslims of the period after the middle of the seventh century. A similar tale was told of the monk Malchus, written by Jerome: Malchus renounced the world as a young man and left his home in Nisibis to live among other desert monks in Syria. Captured by Saracens and enslaved, he was eventually liberated when his master was eaten by a lioness, and with his female companion he then reached a Roman military camp safely. Jerome states that he had this account from Malchus himself, a living witness to the events (*Vita Malchi*, in *AS Oct.* IX: 59–69).

48 Variants: Sigalas 1924: 317–319; Theodore of Stoudios: Pitra 1876: 365.ια.

49 The rapacity of soldiers and the threat they posed to civil society was a standard motif in ancient and medieval literature. One version of miracle 6 (see below) concerns a soldier who steals a valuable sword and is likewise presented by later writers (such as John Mauropous: de Lagarde 1882: 133.17) in this light. There is a substantial body of late Roman legislation testifying to the reality as well as the perception of soldiers' impact on civilian affairs. An imperial rescript issued in 527 grants imperial protection to an oratory in Pamphylia from the harm inflicted by soldiers and officers charged with policing the region against brigands (Grégoire 1922: no. 314); several *novellae* or laws issued in respect of reorganising provincial administration in both Asia Minor and provinces such as Palestine and Arabia refer to similar problems, and in particular the illegal imposition on local people by soldiers and other officials of extra prestations, hospitality and similar demands (Just., *Nov.*, 28, § 4, pr., for Hellenopontus, a. 535; 29, § 3, for Paphlagonia, a. 535; 30, § 7. 2, for Cappadocia, a. 536); Justinian's Edict VIII, issued in 548, refers explicitly to the abuses of soldiers in the provinces: Just., *Edict.* VIII, §§ 2, 3, a. 548 (in this case, in the Pontic diocese).

behind him, protested with loud cries about whose stolen hen it was. [63] Still the audacious fellow did not give it up, but, showing contempt for the martyr, killed it and consumed it! Yet the lamentation from the punishment surpasses the pleasure of the feast, for the punishment is not corporal injury but the chastisement of loss. For he suddenly saw the horse he owned, a horse well-suited to warfare, lying dead. Know the unyielding force of the martyr's anger! – yet learn of his unsurpassable kindness, which reconsidered the soldier: for, after experiencing his wrath, he bought two larger hens to replace the one, and came bearing them to the church. Carrying the saddle of the dead horse upon his shoulders as well, he accused the martyr thus: 'For one stolen hen a warhorse was demanded of me in return – behold, I lay down before you twice the value of what was stolen, may you now make amends for injury done to me through my horse.'[50] The martyr received these words neither in enmity nor in anger, but conquering soldierly harshness with sympathy once again tempered it with a certain wondrous gentleness in his charity towards the deed.

A little while earlier a person had arrived leading a horse. Appearing before the guardian of the holy precinct, he [the martyr] foretold that, 'A certain soldier with such-and-such an appearance will come. When you take the hen from him, give him in return the horse he needs.' And, as a result, when the traveller arrived at the church and went off, a cavalryman once more, one could see a sight filled with much joy, [64] tears were turned to joy, grief to pleasure, condemnation to reverence, blame to thanksgiving. Hear now in addition another wonderful deed.

See Haldon 1999: 145–147, 234–247; Erdkamp 1998: 84–140 with further literature as well as sources relevant to both ancient and medieval society.

50 In all periods loss of a horse, an expensive item, could be disastrous for the soldier, and was well understood by all. Horses were provided for cavalry soldiers by the state in the period before the middle of the seventh century, and for some soldiers thereafter, and their loss other than in the line of duty was a charge to the soldier; in the provinces soldiers were by the eighth century responsible for providing their own mount, so the loss was likewise a serious matter. See Jones 1964: 663; 834–9.

[Miracle 3] Sigalas 1921: 64.5–65.9; Delehaye 1925a: 62–63 [13][51]

There were some moneychangers[52] who together owned a workshop,[53] one acting as master, the other as servant. They possessed a particular valuable silver paten.[54] Now someone stole this, unseen, while they were engaged in their transactions. The master suspected the servant, and in no wise did he change his opinion about this, with the result that, in desperation, albeit unwillingly, the servant consulted with fortune tellers and investigated every sort of superstition. In the end, lamenting bitterly, he took refuge and prayed night and day in the inner atrium of the martyr's church. The martyr, heeding his supplications, informed him of the perpetrator of the theft. But since he could not unambiguously recognise the man from this information, the martyr solved his difficulties in this respect once more. 'Get up at dawn,' he said, 'and go a little way outside the church, and firmly seize the first person you meet! And you'll find what you seek from him. But, when you have recovered what was stolen, let the thief go without any charge.'[55] Having given these instructions, he went to the false accuser and brought together at the same time both him and the man who had had the effrontery to commit the theft [65], carrying the paten in his arms, for he had already spent a good deal of time going about presenting it for sale to those who were interested. So the man, who was convinced by the earlier revelations of the martyr, seized the thief. The latter, pricked in his conscience, said immediately, 'The paten you seek – behold, I bring it to you. But be satisfied with its recovery, for you neither expected nor hoped

51 Variants: Sigalas 1924: 319–321; Delehaye 1925a: 62–64; and cf. Theodore of Stoudios, in Pitra 1876: 365.ια. Compare this tale with a similar episode in Cyril of Scythopolis' *Vita S. Sabae*, 184.21–185.16 (§78) (*BHG* 1608; *CPG* 3: 7536; see Sigalas 1921: 92); with a somewhat differently nuanced story about the theft of a silver plate in a miracle of St Menas: Duffy and Bourbouhakis 2003: 71–73; and with *Vita Theod. Syk.*, §34.

52 *Argyropratai*: see Hendy 1985: 242–251; ἀργυροπράτης meant literally a seller of silver (Lat. *argentarius*). In the fifth and sixth centuries it referred also, and usually, to a moneylender, since those who worked with silver could generally also operate in this capacity; and while *argyropratai* from other major cities were known, those from the capital were particularly wealthy and also had political influence. Some commissioned the building of churches, for example: see Barnish 1985 on the wealthy banker Julius Argentarius.

53 ἐργαστήριον. Literally a workshop, but it could refer to any place of business, such as the premises where financial or monetary exchange transactions took place. See *ODB* 1: 726–727.

54 δίσκος. See Lampe 1961: 375. s.v. (3).

55 Cf. mir. 11 and Sigalas 1921: 92 on Theodore's reputation as a revealer of lost or stolen property.

for this, and do not bring about my own ruination through your success.'
With these words, he persuaded him. And in such ways the martyr shows
his love of mankind even to the unjust.

Next you will hear a tale of soldierly ferocity.

[Miracle 4] Sigalas 1921: 65.10–68.5; Delehaye 1925a: 63 [14][56]

Two martyrs,[57] both of similar character and disposition to the martyr
Theodore, shared a single church as their abode.[58] Some notables of the
region deposited some women's jewellery with the God-fearing man who
had been placed in charge of the precinct. After some time had passed,
those who had made the deposit sought the valuables from the pious man,
and while he admitted that he had received the deposit, he said he did not
know what had happened to it. For when he looked in his treasury he did
not find what he had placed there. To those who sought their property, this
seemed to be a false excuse and a pretence for fraud. But this was not the
case, for the man had a servant, the son of a wicked father, and the boy was
persuaded [66] by his father to steal the aforementioned item and hand it
over to him. Those who had been deprived of their property resorted to the
assistance of the local official, denounced the holy old man and had him
dragged out of the martyrs' church and brought him before the authorities
in the town. This caused great astonishment among those who saw it. For
it was on the one hand unusual for everyone for him ever to be seen in a
court of justice, and more unusual still for the man to appear in public on
such a charge. So what did this unjustly maligned man do? He called upon
the sympathy of the two martyrs whom he served, and together with them
he called also upon the noble martyr Theodore to devise some positive
outcome. Which indeed these martyrs secretly did. For they sought out the

---

56 Variants: Sigalas 1924: 321–324.

57 It is not clear who this pair might be: George and Merkourios, fellow soldier-saints; or
perhaps Sergius and Bacchus.

58 The notion that saints dwelt in their churches was generally accepted, an important
point in relation to debates about whether saints had a real physical existence. For most
hagiographers and their audiences the answer was positive. Thus in miracles of St Artemius,
a collection written in the second half of the seventh century in Constantinople, for example,
the saint is referred to as living in his crypt or walking through the church in more than a
simply metaphorical way (although it is also understood that he was no ordinary mortal): see
Nesbitt and Crisafulli 1997: mir. 32, 34, 37, and 4. Such issues were part of a much wider
debate. See Dagron 1992 and Déroche 1993.

author of the wicked deed by night, and as though appearing in a court, they themselves played the roles of both plaintiffs and judge, approved the charge against him, and themselves urged that he make full restitution. The accused saw that one of those present was as an armed man, and thought that he stretched out his sword against him, and he heard this man referred to by the name of Theodore by the two, who importuned him not to be vexed, for they said that everything he demanded, the accused would do.

Such was the outcome of events resulting from the first aggravation of the martyrs. Yet since [67] the accused did not improve in his behaviour, they appeared once again and threatened him even more harshly than before. But as the deadline for the holy old man to repay the loss arrived, approaching with even greater anger, the two of them pretended to be about to rain blows upon the accused. The warrior himself, not holding back, with his outstretched right hand pierced the side of the incorrigible fellow with his sword. So what did the wounded man do?[59] Unable to withstand the pain of the blow he quickly called his neighbours together and requested, with tears and with many groans, that they carry him in their arms as quickly as possible and leave him in the middle of the church. And when this was done, while the worthy priest laboured and dealt with the court, the thief, in a great assembly of those who had gathered at word of the unusual sight, confessed that he alone was responsible for the crime, and asked those who would recover the stolen item to come to him or go to the house to take it themselves, and that the priest be quickly released from blame, of which he was unjustly suspected.

You have learned how the martyr knew the right time to employ military harshness, how he strikes those who do not heed his exhortations. But do not disregard how much mercy he showed them in such matters. For after [68] the stolen object was revealed, the offender's pains were straight away relieved, so that he who was carried in the arms of others returned on his own feet, restored to health.

Would you like to know another tale of sympathy surpassing all bounds?

---

59 ὁ πληγείς, i.e. both 'stricken' and 'astonished'.

[Miracle 5] Sigalas 1921: 68.6–69.5; Delehaye 1925a: 65 [16][60]

There was a certain person living in great poverty, burdened with many debts from loans and suffering from the implacable demands for payment from his creditors, but with no resources from which to repay them. Seeing the silver candelabra for illuminating the church, he conceived an idea that, while it was wicked in its implementation, yet in its choice of what was intended entailed a justification. He implored that forbearing and compassionate martyr[61] to go along with him to steal one of the fittings, so that he could realise its value by selling it; through this sale he hoped he would be able not only to return twice the value of the fitting but also to pay back what he owed his creditors and relieve his own penury. When he had spoken these words as though the martyr were standing beside him, and being permitted to do this with an unseen nod, he dares to carry out the deed, and through the martyr's collaboration he escapes the notice of all those looking around. The business of his sale went well, so that in a short time the man returned with a great deal of wealth, went directly to the sacred precinct and personally admitted that he had committed the deed, and personally attested to the compassion of the martyr, with whose aid he fulfilled his promise.

[69] Behold, even though the deed was lawless and though its collaborator was he who was wronged [i.e. the martyr], though sacrilege was dared, yet still there was no blame for the deed. For while the source of his wealth was wicked, yet he who shares in it is without reproach. You will learn next from what I will tell you what manner of fatherly disposition the martyr possessed.

[Miracle 6] Sigalas 1921: 69.6–70.12; Delehaye 1925a: 66 [17][62]

Someone brought a beautiful sword decorated with gold (to the church).[63] A boy happened to see it lying on one of the altars, and being seduced by its

---

60 Variants: Sigalas 1924: 324–326.

61 i.e. St Theodore.

62 Variants: Sigalas 1924: 327–329; cf. Theodore of Stoudios, Pitra 1876: 365.ιβ. Miracles 6 and 7, as Sigalas 1921: 95–96 noted, were taken up by Eustratius in his text on the body and the soul: *CPG* 3: 7522; Eustratius, ed. van Deun 2006 (Constas 2002; Beck 1959: 411).

63 In a different version the tale concerns two soldiers, rather than a boy: Sigalas 1924: 328.14–329.16.

beauty went up to it innocently, wishing to take it. So how did the martyr both sport with the child in a fatherly way and give up this new acquisition? The boy placed his right hand on the sword and the martyr allowed him to take it. But as he thought he held it and seemingly closed his grip around it, as soon as the sword began to come through, the grill held his hand fast; yet when he let go of what he had taken his hand was released from its bonds. He tried again to take it and again his hand was held fast. And so, in the simplicity of his years, he entreated the martyr, saying to him: [70] 'Let me have it, holy father, let your servant have the object. For what use is a sword to you? Are you going to sacrifice a hen or a lamb? Or anything else like this? Grant me this gift, like a good father.' And then, saying many similar words, while he let go of it, he was also very sad not to leave in possession of what he desired. Then the martyr appeared to the priest, and informed him who the boy was and whence he came, and that he had charmed him exceedingly with his words. 'So then, do you summon him, and fulfill that which he desires.' And so in accordance with the innocence of his age the child carried the sword off as his reward and left, not so much blessed on its account as through the paternal affection shown to him by the martyr. See how he was gentle and mild when necessary, but once again how he was harsh when he needed to be.

[Miracle 7] Sigalas 1921: 70.13–71.9; Delehaye 66–67 [18][64]

While the annual feastday for the martyr was being celebrated someone made an offering of gold and entrusted it to one of the people involved in the festival. But when he who had received the gold began to deny this, the man who had been deprived of it ran in tears to the church, pleading that the celebration should not be for him alone a cause for grief. So the martyr appeared to him through a dream, saying, 'Desist from your grieving and sit quietly near the church and I will reveal the cunning of those sought by you.' After two or three days, the man who had denied knowledge of the gold came running along of his own accord, and in the midst of people from all over he was suspended in the air itself [71] and confessed the truth, and as though compelled by blows, he said that the offering remained untouched, beseeching everyone to join in his entreaties for the alleviation of his suffering. As a result the first man recovered all that he had offered,

---

64 Variants: Sigalas 1924: 330–331 (note that the line numbers accompanying the text in Sigalas' edition are incorrect on p. 331).

while the second experienced the instant cessation of his pains and went off suffering nothing more, indeed he gained not a little profit from his chastisement, for thereafter he led a life of great piety. Such is the martyr's comportment in the case of the vexations of others. Now behold again how he acts in matters that concern himself.

[Miracle 8] Sigalas 1921: 71.10–72.1; Delehaye 1925a: 67 [19][65]

A gang of wicked men plotted to steal some very beautiful liturgical vessels.[66] And the first thing they did towards this undertaking was to fabricate keys to the doors and to think up every sort of evil artifice. Having lain in wait until evening, gathering together such items as they were able to take, they carried them off, and thought to open up the doors. But when they went out to set off on their way they could not stop running around, until the doorkeepers of the church arose and denounced those impious thieves to the supervisor[67] in charge of the church's contents. So what did he do? He investigated in detail everything that had been done and when he learned that the men had been overwhelmed by such a loss of vision and blindness that they could take only what they could carry beneath their tunics, he released them, commanded by the martyr, who even ordered that they be given some necessary victuals.[68]

[72] Let us not pass over another example of his love for mankind.

[Miracle 9] Sigalas 1921: 72.2–16; Delehaye 1925a: 67–68 [20][69]

A soldier entered the holy precinct on horseback, and without a servant. Leading the horse to one side, he tethered it to a column and, calling out to the martyr, 'I entrust the care of this horse to you', he went into the church and offered up the prayer for which he had come. But when, having

---

65 Variants: Sigalas 1924: 331–332. Note the similarity between this account and the last miracle in the miracles of Euthymius in the *Vita Euthymii*, 81 (§59) by Cyril of Scythopolis. For the topos of thieves or other miscreants attempting to escape but being held back and running around in circles until discovered, compare, e.g., *Vita Theod. Syk.*, §34.

66 In Theodore's church.

67 Probably the *skeuophylax* is meant here. Thanks to Alice-Mary Talbot for this suggestion.

68 Cf. Gen. 19. 11 (and 2 Kings 6. 18) for biblical parallels.

69 Variants: Sigalas 1924: 332–333.

completed this, he went back to his mount, the horse had gone off with another soldier who was galloping away at great speed. But the latter, having begged it of the martyr, did this out of poverty, not being able to buy a horse. At this the soldier who had lost his horse accused the martyr and demanded back the horse he had entrusted to him, and he too described in exaggerated terms his own poverty, swearing that he would not step outside the church until he recovered his lost horse. Receiving this plea favourably, the martyr commanded the steward of the precinct to give the soldier a horse from among those that had been brought as offerings, and not to seek out the animal that had been driven off nor, if it should reappear, to retrieve it owing to the poverty of the man who had taken it.[70]

Come, then, and listen to yet another even more wondrous miracle worked through the kindly power of the martyr.

[Miracle 10] Sigalas 1921: 72.17–73.11; Delehaye 1925a: 68–69 [21][71]

A certain fellow who was bringing an ox as a sacrifice to the martyr took up lodging in one of the villages along the road, and asked to buy fodder with which to feed the sacrificial animal.[72] [73] But someone offered what was requested without payment and asked that part of the sacrifice be credited to him. Now the man bringing the gift came to the church and when he arrived the martyr told the priest not to accept the sacrificed offering only from the man who brought it, for he had a partner. When this was announced the man became displeased, and complained indignantly that he was not able to understand until, examining everything closely, he recalled the man who had given him the small gift of fodder. So then he invited him too to share in the sacrificial offering, while the martyr received the gift from them both. Such is his concern, that nothing be without reward for him who acts in faith.

---

70 In this, as in several other miracles in this collection, the saint is credited with a partic-ularly charitable mercy towards sinners and those who have in some way or other harmed others. This is not an uncommon attribute: compare with the somewhat more striking account of St Menas, who chastises but then pardons a murderer for his crime after first bringing the murder victim back to life (and reassembling his dismembered corpse): Duffy and Bourbouhakis 2003: 68–60.

71 Variants: Sigalas 1924: 333–334.

72 Cf. the tenth miracle in the seventh-century collection, below (Text 4).

Listen now to what was most illustriously bestowed upon the martyr on behalf of others through the divine power working through him.

[Miracle 11] Sigalas 1921: 73.12–74.2; Delehaye 1925a: 69 [22][73]

Just as he takes the sickle against the thieves, as in the book of the

---

73 Variants: Sigalas 1924: 334–336; note esp. the variant of Theodore of Stoudios, Pitra 1876: 364.ι. Of the several different versions one, composed in or shortly after the last decade of the ninth century, is much longer (Sigalas 1924: 335.6–336.14) and includes the story of a person of status whose servant is carried off. The man seeks high and low but fails to find the servant and eventually appeals to St Theodore for help. He spends three days and nights in the martyr's church without any sign of Theodore, but eventually during the third night he appears to the man in a dream and, responding to the man's complaint that he had not come earlier, explains that he was unable to come before because he had been called away by God to Constantinople to attend the passing away and ascent to heaven of Joseph the Hymnographer (d. ca. 886: see *PmbZ* #3454, #23510; Beck 1959: 601–602). He then tells the man to worry no longer about his servant, but to go to a certain place, where he will find him. This he does, and the story ends with his offering praise and glory to God and to His servant Theodore. A similar account of St Theodore is told by Cyril of Scythopolis in his *Life* of St Saba, where it is the latter on whose account Theodore must be absent: see *Vita S. Sabae*, 184–185 (§78). The story is interesting additionally because it suggests that by the time of writing the assumption that a saint might bilocate was not common, although it had been an important issue at an earlier period. In the later seventh century Anastasios of Sinai argued that, since neither saints nor ordinary mortals have a physical presence after death, the soul of the ordinary human loses all its powers of memory, self-identity and recognition, and must await the Last Judgement in this state of limbo. But while those of the saints do retain a degree of consciousness, it is the heavenly angels who represent them on earth, taking on their customary apparel and appearance in order to demonstrate the power of the Holy Spirit to those who inhabit the world of mortals. In partial proof of his argument, Anastasios notes that the same saint has often been observed in different places at the same time (see Anastasius Sin., ed. Richard and Munitiz 2006: qu. 19. 8; 20. 1; 21. 4). Another case is recounted in the miracles of Artemius – to name but one hagiographical example – where the saint is made to say on at least two occasions (mir. 31 and 40) that he has been absent on, or must hurry away to attend, other business, as in this version of the 11th miracle of St Theodore. See discussion in Dagron 1992: 62–63; Déroche 1993: 113–114. Eustratius (author of the *Life* of the patriarch Eutychius), in his treatise on the nature of the soul and the relationship it bears to the body after death (ed. van Deun 2006), sets out to refute 'rationalist' arguments in a debate that was particularly relevant to the question of the plausibility of the miracles performed by, as well as the causal powers ascribable to, the saints whose deeds were extolled in the various miracle collections. This was an explicit attempt to provide a theologically grounded explanation for such miracles, in which divine intervention and the direct mediation of God through the saints were fundamental elements. See also n. 77 below.

God-bearing Zacharias,[74] and uses the same weapon also against servants who run away, thus he exposes everywhere the evil deeds of some and binds the feet of others.[75] And to whichever of his churches anyone might have recourse, whether seeking information about stolen property or requesting that the flight of slaves be checked, it suffices for that person in either case to take a small wax seal and to store it away in his home, through which he [the martyr] will in the one case bring the thieves to subjection and in the other will likewise restore the runaways.[76] [74] For each deed has a wondrous proof, so let us proceed, if you agree, to another proof.[77]

[Miracle 12] Sigalas 1921: 74.3–76.6; Delehaye 1925a: 69 [23]–71 [25][78]

The city that until today guards the imperial scepter unharmed,[79] that city that is the head of the civilised world, as a city of men often falls foul of many afflictions, but as a city beloved of God always escapes danger. When, therefore, the recent conflagration overtook it,[80] what wonder does he, that

74 See Zechariah 5. 1–2. Zechariah was known as the 'sickle-seer' or 'sickle-beholder' because of his sixth vision, in which he saw a flying scroll in the shape of a sickle that would sweep away thieves and blasphemers. In later biblical exegesis, and as here, the sickle was often interpreted literally as well as metaphorically.

75 An attribute reflecting contemporary views and problems related to the control of servile labour and represented in much imperial legislation of the fourth–sixth centuries. See Jones 1964: 792–812 for a general overview; and on the return of runaway *coloni* see *Nov. Val.* 31.

76 The wax seal probably contained an impression of the image of the saint or was in some other way associated with the saint's presence, and bore several functions in such a context: see Hahn 1990: 93; and cf. miracle 16 of St Artemius in which a wax seal plays an important role in transmitting the intercessory power of the saint: Nesbitt and Crisafulli 1997: 107–109.

77 Cf. John 14. 11. While acceptance of the miraculous was widespread and probably reflects the cultural norm, debate about the nature of the miraculous in the context of relations between the human and divine was a constant. In the sixth and seventh centuries in particular the tension between what we might dub the 'rationalist' and 'populist' perspectives was lively, although it was certainly a feature of Christian theological reflection from the beginning. See n. 73 above; and Constas 2002; Dagron 1992; on the sixth- and seventh-century debate: Haldon 1997b: 44–56; note also Dal Santo 2011: 129–138; and in general Kaldellis 2014.

78 Variants: Sigalas 1924: 337–338; cf. Theodore of Stoudios, in Pitra 1876: 365.ιγ.

79 Constantinople.

80 Generally understood as the fire of the year 465, but as we have seen (above, pp. 24–25), an earlier fire is also possible. There is in any case some disagreement about the date of the fire of 465, in light of the contradictory reports of the sources. See Janin 1937: 139.

same miracle-worker, once again bring to pass? He had formerly a small and insignificant church in the city.[81] But the church was connected to a very large and distinguished courtyard, displaying the greatness of the founder in every aspect of its construction.[82] Now although the latter numbered among those possessing earthly dignities, yet he took even greater pride in his zeal for the faith and preferred to be called a servant of God rather than father of emperors, and to hear that he shared the inheritance of the martyrs rather than the throne of the consuls. And other such accomplishments adorned this man – the achievement of monastic self-restraint, a consular generosity with regard to alms, sympathy for those in need and afflicted, liberal in his patronage [75] and pleasing to God in all things; and while there is not time to laud such things in detail now, what has been said in the foregoing is sufficient for the present as evidence of his conduct. For as the fire encircled the courtyard on all sides, gushing forth like a river, it all but outdid the scale of the fiery furnace of Babylon in its upward rush, and there was nowhere it did not spread with great speed. For since the walls connected to the roofs, they caught fire from one to the other, and the buildings and their inhabitants were all consumed together, livestock and their owners, all were completely engulfed, and in vain were streams of water expended from all directions. Then indeed the aforementioned man, seeing that the disaster surpassed human aid, yet in the hope that comes from faith, and not being willing to despair of salvation, but rather in imitation of Abraham and reasoning, as Paul said, 'that God can raise from the dead,'[83] he halted the hard labour of his servants and stopped them carrying water. And standing in the middle of the flames engulfing the building and raising his hands to

81 Built in 412. See Janin 1969: 152 with sources; Sigalas 1921: 99–100.

82 Although Chrysippos, as usual, does not name this person, it is assumed to have been a certain Sphoracius, a former *comes domesticorum* of the east who held a consulship in the year 452 and who was credited with the construction of a more magnificent church for St Theodore on the same site. See *PLRE* 2: 1026–1027 (Fl. Sphoracius 3); Just., *Nov.* 3. 1; *Patria CP.* iii, 30 (225–226). A later version of the miracle names the man as 'Staurakios (or Sparakios), a certain *patrikios*': Sigalas 1924: 337.10–11. For the district of Constantinople named for him – τὰ Σφωρακίου – see Janin 1964: 428–429. A brief inscription preserved in the *Greek Anthology* i, 6 records: 'On the church of St Theodore in the district of Sphorakios: Sphorakios having escaped from a fire built this temple to the martyr.' Sphoracius seems to have been buried there, according to the next entry (i, 7): 'Sphorakios, Anatolios your nephew rejoiced in repaying during your life your generosity in bringing him up, and now that you are dead ever pays you grateful honour. So that he found for you a new honour, and laid you in the temple you yourself built.'

83 Cf. Acts 26. 8.

heaven, he called upon the champion who was hard at hand [i.e. the martyr], beseeching him on the one hand to help in winning God's intercession, and on the other for him to become a wall of protection for all those in the house. And employing such language, immediately events conformed to his words. [76] For the martyr was observed by many moving up and down and leaping from one place to another, checking the ferocity of the conflagration with his hands.[84] And, in addition to this spectacle, confirmation followed from their experience. For while the fire caught the beams and covered them in flames, still they did not burn. Everything round about was destroyed, yet the whole house, like an invincible bastion, remained alone untouched and free from all harm.[85]

[77] The tales I have recounted above number twelve, and what more holy number than this could anyone find? For this is the number of the sons of

84 While there is some discussion about the exact date of the fire in question, and leaving to one side the miraculous intervention of the saint, the account here bears comparison with actual events reported in other sources. In the fifth-century *Vita Marciani* (Marcian was a priest and *oikonomos* of the Hagia Sophia, fl. ca. 450–472), composed by a near-contemporary, Sergius (Snee 1998: 157, 164–175; see also Saradi 1996), there is an account of the fire of 465 in which Marcian is described as climbing onto the roof of the church with the holy books and thus saving it from the flames (see Snee 1998: 170). More interestingly still, the Alan *magister militum* Aspar was reported to have actively fought the fire, organizing a bucket-chain, for example (such as is alluded to in this miracle of St Theodore): see *PLRE* II: 164–169 (Fl. Ardabur Aspar), with 167 for sources and literature relating to the fire. This was in stark contrast to the emperor Leo I, who fled the city during the fire: Dawes and Baynes 1948: 33–34 and 79, note (the *Life* of Daniel the Stylite, caps 45–46). One wonders whether such stories influenced Chrysippos' account, if it was written after 465.

85 A later version included the following additional concluding section (see Sigalas 1921: 76, note to 76.6; and 101): 'And there is in this regard something else even more remarkable. For this generous martyr, neglecting the survival from the fire's destruction of his own church, transferred all his succour to the man's house, so that in some way not only was the fire itself not to be feared, but the martyr's wishes were respected because of his great affection towards the man, the latter having neither entreated nor hesitated to offer his house as a ransom for another's. So blessed be the man on account of all that has been said; let him in addition be blessed yet more because of his good will in these matters, for he never ceases continuously to trumpet abroad the Benefactor. And instead of a small church he built for him a great one, instead of an aged one a brand-new one, instead of a humble one a church filled with precious objects, thus multiplying his repayment many times over and in so multiplying it continued to offer daily gifts and repayments. But while many events – indeed an even greater number than these – attract my attention, yet bearing in mind what I said before about not immoderately extending the account, I will throw back the greater part of these streams and fence off the entrance just as in a winter torrent, knowing that the number of tales itself no longer excuses me from proceeding with the matter of the eulogy'.

Jacob, the number of the precious stones of the priestly robe,[86] such is the choir of the prophets, those who announced to us the shorter prophecies,[87] and such is the assembly of the apostles. And so it is fitting to set forth also the distinctive honour of this number in the crown of the martyr.

Come, let us now say the following to him, since he stands close to us and hearkens: Most illustrious of martyrs, put forth your armament on our behalf. Wage war against the temptation that marches against us in many guises, [78] for here you must serve too as a soldier, especially there where the sceptre of your king is present, here you must also be continuously near at hand, or rather in this world you should sit always in the palace. You watch over Bethlehem also, you keep guard around the altar of Golgotha, you lead the choir in the bridal chamber of the Church of the Resurrection, you dance on the Mount of Olives, but you also share a meal in the upper room of Sion.[88] Yet alongside those who dance with you, draw up in battle array against the devil's devices against us, for we are beset by many opportunities for sin. Assemble in sleepless watch over us, all you guardsmen and allies of Christ, set your defences against those attacks of sinfulness among us, you guardsmen and allies of Christ; say now to the king, 'Awake, why do you sleep, Lord? *Arise and do not cast us off forever.*' For the divine poet David interceded of old with such words on our behalf.[89]

Now I have the opportunity to bring yet another entreaty before you, you [79] who act always with God-given courage in heroic feats, or rather I have the opportunity to bring you the same entreaty and request: grant me what was promised by those who encouraged me to undertake this euology: grace in speech, enlightenment in thought, the gift that comes from knowledge of God, the liberty of speech through the proclamation of the Gospel.[90] For you can accomplish all things, Christ permitted you, his saints, to bestow every gift, so as he is glorified among all the saints, let the glory and the power be with Him for ever and ever. Amen.

---

86 The twelve precious stones were part of the breastpiece of Aaron, the first chief priest, and symbolised the twelve tribes: see Exod. 28. 17–21. In Christian priestly vestments they represented the twelve apostles, but could also invoke the twelve gates and twelve foundation stones of the new Jerusalem. For late antique/Byzantine images of this garb in its OT context: Kominko 2013: 123–126.

87 The 'twelve minor prophets' (Hosea to Malachi).

88 By the fourth century the name Sion referred in Christian usage to the south-westerly ridge of Jerusalem, and the site of the Last Supper. See Mare 1992a: (C) with literature.

89 Paraphrasing Ps. 44. 24–27.

90 Cf., e.g., Ephes. 3. 8–12.

Text 2: *BHG* 1761, ed. Delehaye 1909: 127–135; 1925: 29–39[91]

The passion of St Theodore the Recruit

[127] 1. The emperors Maximianus and Maximinus,[92] in thrall to the devil, sent throughout all of their empire an edict against all the followers of the true religion of Christ that those who tasted food that had been defiled[93] would be spared and that those who spoke against this were to be surrendered to the courts. At this time the holy Theodore was conscripted for military service in the east and, together with many other recruits, was assigned to a legion entitled the *legio Marmaritarum*[94] under the *praepositus* Bringas.[95] This legion was billeted in the city of Amasia[96] in the province of Helenopontus.[97] About four miles from the city of Euchaïta was a dense wood, and there was an ancient serpent that had become a

91 Page numbers in square brackets in Texts 3 and 4 are to the edition in Delehaye 1909.

92 C. Galerius Valerius Maximianus (to be distinguished from his predecessor Herculius Maximianus, Augustus in the west from 286–305: *PLRE* 1:316 and W. Ensslin, in *RE* XIV [1930] 2486–2516) was Caesar from 293–305 and Augustus from 305–311, see *PLRE* 1:574–575 and W. Ensslin, in *RE* XIV [1930] 2516–2528. Maximinus (See *PLRE* 1: 579–580 [Galerius Valerius Maximinus Daia 12]) was Caesar in the east from 305, and was proclaimed Augustus by his troops in 309/310.

93 I.e. offered in sacrifice. See p. 59 above.

94 A unit entitled *cohors tertia Valeria Marmantarum* is listed under the command of the *Dux Syriae et Euphratensis Syriae* in the first half of the fifth century: *Not. Dig., Or.* xxxiii (ed. Seeck 1876: 70); a *noumeron Marmaritôn* is mentioned in the martyrdom of St Christopher in Lycia under Decius: *BHG* 309; ed. Usener 1886: 56. 13.

95 The title and rank of *praepositus* had several overlapping meanings in the late Roman military hierarchy, in general terms equivalent to a senior tribune or *comes*. See W. Ensslin in *RE, Suppl.* VIII, 548–555. The name Bringas/Briggas is not found in late Roman texts but is attested in the Byzantine period from the tenth century: see *PmbZ* # 2352: Joseph Briggas. One wonders whether a tenth-century redactor of this version of the text introduced this particular name deliberately.

96 For Amasia see above. A number of units were based there at different times: French 1992; 1996.

97 After the reign of Diocletian (284–305), and by 308, the province of Pontus (which had in the middle of the third century been administered as a sub-region of Galatia before becoming a separate province again by 279 CE) was renamed Diospontus. It included six cities (Amasia, Ibora, Zela, Andrapa, Amisus and Sinope), but was again renamed, as Helenopontus, at some point after 325 and before the end of the reign of Constantine I in 337. See Mitchell 1993: 158–160; Jones 1954. It was given two further cities after this: at some point in the reign of Anastasius (491–518), as we have seen, Euchaïta was created as a city out of the territory of Amasia; and in the early sixth century *Synecdemus* of Hierocles, a secular list of cities and provinces, a settlement named *Saltus Zalichen* is listed for the province,

dragon there and that had made its lair in the grove, and had slaughtered many of those who had passed along that road. Now it happened that before his martyrdom the holy Theodore also passed along that road, and when he espied him, the dragon charged down upon him, hissing. The noble soldier of Christ, crossing himself and hurling his spear, pierced its head and slew it, and thus the whole road was freed from that day forth.[98]

[128] 2. But when the blessed Theodore was brought to the *praepositus* Bringas and was ordered to offer sacrifice to the gods, that true soldier of Christ, faithful to God and filled with the Holy Spirit, standing in the midst of the legion, replied, 'I am a Christian and I have not accepted the command to offer sacrifice to false idols.' The *praepositus* Bringas said in reply, 'Now you shall listen to me, Theodore, and take your arms, and since you have been enrolled in military service, sacrifice to the immortal gods and obey the invincible emperors.' But saint Theodore said in response, 'I serve my own emperor and I cannot serve another.' The *praepositus* Bringas answered, 'But all those standing around are Christians, and they serve.' But Theodore answered, saying, 'Each knows how he serves. But I serve my king and heavenly Lord, God, and his only-begotten son Jesus Christ.' Poseidonius the *ducenarius*,[99] who was standing by, asked, 'So your god also has a son?' to which saint Theodore replied, 'Yes, he does have a son, the Word of truth, through whom he made all things.'[100] So he said to him, 'Can we know him?' Saint Theodore replied, 'Would that God would bestow such understanding on you as to recognise him.' And Poseidonius said, 'But if we recognise him, surely we cannot abandon our earthly emperor and go to him?' and saint Theodore answered 'There is nothing that prevents you from abandoning the darkness and the brief access that you have to your ephemeral and mortal earthly emperor and, going over to God, the living and eternal king and lord, in order to serve

---

probably to be identified with a city of Leontopolis mentioned in Just., *Nov.* 28 (a. 535). See Honigmann 1939; Jones 1971: 514–521.

98 As noted above (Chapter 2, pp. 29–31), this paragraph about the dragon – from 'About four miles from the city of Euchaïta', to 'the whole road was freed from that day forth', seems somewhat awkwardly inserted at this point.

99 In the fourth–seventh centuries a senior subaltern officer, the next grade up from *centenarius* (the equivalent of the older *centurio*). See Jones 1964: 626, 634, 674–676. For the ranks and hierarchy in the various types of military formation in the late Roman period see the older but still valuable discussions in Grosse 1915; 1920: 127–138, 144–145.

100 The relatively neutral Christological position expressed here gives no clue as to when this particular *passio* was composed.

Him as I do.' The *praepositus* Bringas then said, 'Let us give him a few days in order to take stock with himself and come to the right decision.'[101]

[129] 3. While he took this time to think, the authorities made a great clamour about other Christians in the city, whom they likewise arrested and took away. St Theodore followed and called gently to them, instructing them in the path to salvation and in perseverance, that they might not deny Christ the king. When they had been locked up, he waited for an opportune moment and during the night set fire to the temple of the mother of the gods. But he was seen by someone and, when he was denounced, the book-keeper Cronides, terrified at what had been done, seized him and brought him before the magistrate Publius Straton, informing him in these words that, 'This pest, a conscript who recently came into our city, set fire to the temple of the mother of the gods, and insulted our gods. So I apprehended him and have brought him to your highness, so that in accordance with the divine edict of the emperors of the earthly kingdom he may be punished for his outrageous deeds.' The magistrate, having summoned the *praepositus* Bringas, said to him, 'Did you give him permission to set fire to the temple of the mother of our gods?' In reply he said, 'I exhorted him frequently, and gave him some time to think matters over and make sacrifice. Yet even if he has come to this, he has still shown contempt for the imperial commands; but you are the magistrate.' And the magistrate, sitting on his rostrum, ordered Theodore to be brought before him.[102]

4. When he had been brought in, he [the magistrate] said to him, 'Why did you set a fire instead of sacrificing to the goddess with incense and libations?' Theodore said, 'I do not deny what I have done. I set wood alight in order that stone be burned, and such was your goddess that [130] fire can touch her.' Then the magistrate ordered that he be beaten, saying, 'My tender words have rendered you bolder in your presumption. But when you are suffering from the most bitter of torments, you will be

101 Compare the very similar account – which Delehaye 1909: 23–25 argues was taken from this text or a closely related version of the passion of Theodore – in the *Passio* of S. Theagenes (*BHG* 749: Hieron et socii): ed. Franchi De'Cavalieri 1912.

102 The trial and interrogation of the accused are central motifs in all the martyrdom accounts, and reflect – more or less accurately, depending upon the time and place of composition – in broad outline (but sometimes in detail), but with amplifications and dramatic exaggeration, the process of a Roman trial. See Detoraki 2014: 67–69; Delehaye 1921: 171–218.

compelled to obey the commands of the emperors.' And Theodore replied, 'Your word is neither persuasive of the truth nor will your tortures prevail over me, even if you make them yet more terrible in order that I do not endure in the hope of future blessings.' The magistrate said, 'Sacrifice to the gods and save yourself from torment.' Theodore replied, 'Those tortures that you inflict are not torments to me, for my Lord and my God stands before my face and will deliver me from your punishments. You do not see him because you do not see with the eyes of the soul.' Thus the magistrate was enraged and, roaring like a lion,[103] ordered him to be thrown into prison, that the door of the prison be sealed and that he be left there, to starve to death.

5. But blessed Theodore was nourished by the Holy Spirit, for that same night the Lord appeared to him, saying *'Take courage, Theodore, for I am with you.*[104] Do not accept either food or drink from these men, for you will have everlasting life with me in heaven.' When he had said these things, he left him, and when the Lord had departed, blessed Theodore began to rejoice and to sing psalms. Moreover, there was a host of angels listening to him. The prison guards [131] arose and rushed to the door of the cell, and saw that the door was closed and the seal intact. But looking through the window they saw a great host dressed in white and singing together with blessed Theodore. Struck with fear, they reported these things to their leader, and he arose and came running to the door of the cell, where he found the chain locked and heard the sound of those singing with Theodore. So he surrounded the cell with soldiers armed with shields, thinking that there were Christians with the blessed Theodore. Yet when he entered, he found no-one other than the servant of God, quite alone and secured in the stocks. And great fear seized him and those with him, so locking the doors again, they departed. Then the magistrate ordered that the blessed man take a crust of bread[105] and a cup of water. But the faithful

---

103 The Christian Roman and later Byzantine view of the lion was ambivalent, drawing on both OT and classical imagery and folklore. While it was seen as a symbol of Christ and of the Christian emperor as victorious rulers, it was also seen as a roaring beast and a symbol of impurity, as in this and many other hagiographical or polemical works. At a slightly later date it was particularly associated with the emperor Leo III and later iconoclast emperors. See *ODB* 2: 1231–1232.

104 See, e.g. Haggai 2. 4; Joshua 1. 9; 1 Kings 2. 2; Deuteronomy 31. 23 etc.

105 The text has *ougkia artou*, i.e. a Roman ounce (= 1/12 of a litre) of bread. The English term 'crust' better conveys the sense intended.

martyr, in accordance with Scriptural verse that *the righteous man shall live by faith*,[106] was not willing to accept any bread from them, saying, 'My lord feeds me.'[107]

6. And the magistrate ordered [Theodore] to be brought before him, and said to him, 'If you are persuaded by me without torture, by the gods, I will write immediately to the emperors, lords of the world, that you should become a high priest [or perhaps a bishop] and receive no ordinary honours; and you will govern jointly with us.' But blessed Theodore, looking up at heaven and crossing himself, said to the tyrant, 'Even if you burn my flesh with fire and destroy me with cunning torments and hand me over to the sword and wild beasts, so long as there is breath in my body I will not deny the [132] name of my Christ.'[108] The magistrate, taking counsel with the *praepositus*, ordered the torturers to hang him up and lacerate his ribs. The *speculatores* lacerated him to such an extent that his ribs were laid bare. But blessed Theodore made no answer to the tyrant, and reciting the psalms, said, *'I will bless the Lord at all times: his praise shall be continually in my mouth.'*[109] The tyrant, amazed at such great endurance in the man, said to the holy martyr, 'Are you not ashamed, most wretched of all men, to place your hopes in a man, and a criminal at that? Have you thus surrendered yourself irrationally to such punishments?' But the blessed martyr said, 'This shame of mine is that of all who call upon the name of my Lord Jesus Christ.' And as the mob was calling out for him to be killed forthwith, the magistrate asked him through a messenger either to sacrifice or be taken away. But the holy martyr, speaking confidently in Christ, said to the tyrant, 'O you most wicked man, filled with every evil, you son of the devil, truly worthy of Satan's work, do you not fear God who gave you this power? For through Him kings reign and monarchs rule the earth,[110] yet you compel me to desert the living God and bow down before lifeless stones?' Then the magistrate said, after much consideration, 'What do you want? To be with

---

106 Rom. 1. 17; cf. Habakkuk 2. 4; Hebrews 10. 38.
107 Cf. Ps. 23. 1; 5.
108 Cf. Hebrews 10.33–36; Matt. 10.32–33. The text has here 'breath in my nostrils'.
109 Ps. 34. 1.
110 A paraphrase of Prov. 8. 15–16: By me kings reign, and princes decree justice. By me nobles become great, and monarchs by me rule over the earth (15: δι' ἐμοῦ βασιλεῖς βασιλεύουσι καὶ οἱ δυνάσται γράφουσι δικαιοσύνην· 16: δι' ἐμοῦ μεγιστᾶνες μεγαλύνονται, καὶ τύραννοι δι' ἐμοῦ κρατοῦσι γῆς). Compare this passage with Text 1, p. 63 above.

us or with your Christ?' To which the holy martyr replied with great joy, 'I have been, I am and will be with my Christ.'[111]

[133] 7. Seeing that he was unable to overcome the man's endurance through torture, the tyrant issued the following judgement against him. 'Theodore, who does not obey the authority of the victorious emperors and the gods, but who believes in Jesus Christ who was crucified under Pontius Pilate, as I hear, by the Jews, he too shall be delivered to fire.'[112] These things happened with great speed, even more quickly than the words were spoken, for the executioners, who had been gathering wood from the workshops and the baths, led him to the place that had been prepared.[113] When the fire had been readied, after removing his clothes and unloosing his belt, he tried to undo his shoes, not doing this earlier because each of the faithful was hastening to be the first to touch his skin, for even before his passion all were coming and touching him. So straight away they placed around him the materials necessary for the fire. But when they went to nail him up, he said 'Leave me as I am; for he who has granted that I may endure the fire unharmed, he will also grant that I endure the fire without the support you provide through the nails.' But while they did not nail him, they bound him. And the martyr, having made the sign of the cross on his forehead, and with his hands tied behind his back, like a distinguished ram chosen from a great flock, was prepared as an offering and as a burnt sacrifice to God.

8. Looking up to heaven, he said, 'Lord God almighty, father of your beloved and blessed son, Jesus Christ, through whom we received knowledge of you, God of powers and all creation and every nation of [134] righteous men who live in your presence! I bless you because you have deemed me worthy, on this day and at this hour, of being numbered among the martyrs in the cup of your Christ at the resurrection of eternal life of body and soul through the immortality of the Holy Spirit, in which I pray to be received favourably before you today as a rich and acceptable sacrifice, just as you, O pure and true God, have beforehand prepared and

111 Cf. Gal. 2. 20; 2 Cor. 5. 15 (and John 14. 18–21).

112 In the *Acta Polycarpi* 13. 1 the Jews are actively involved in preparing the pyre. For the range of punishments described in the martyrologies: Frankfurter 2009; and on the topos of the rejection of the various promises made by the authorities in exchange for their being willing to sacrifice: Delehaye 1921: 257–259, 273–304.

113 From this point in §7 until the final sentence in §8 the text follows almost exactly the *Acta Polycarpi* 13.1–15.2 (320–322).

revealed and now fulfilled. And I praise you accordingly, and bless you through our heavenly high priest Jesus Christ your beloved son. Grant also, Lord, that those recruits who are Christians who have been detained with me will also obtain this prize.'[114] And casting his eyes about him he saw Cleonicus,[115] who had been conscripted along with him, standing in the crowd and weeping, and calling out said, 'Cleonicus, I await you, make haste to join me. We did not desert one another in this mortal life, so let us not be separated from one another in the heavenly life.' When he had finished speaking he again prayed, saying, 'Lord Jesus Christ, mediator between God and men, I thank you, that you have deemed me worthy to win this contest, wherefore glory be to you and with you and power to your Father and to the life-giving Spirit now and for ever and ever.' When he had finished praying, the men tending the pyre lit the flame. But while a great fire was kindled, we to whom it was granted to see beheld a wonder, and were preserved in order to report to others what happened. For the flames took the shape of an arched roof, like a ship's sail filled by the wind, and [135] like a wall surrounded the body of the saint, and it was not so much like flesh burning than a loaf being baked. And we sensed a fragrance, and at last he uttered Amen, and as though disgorging it he released his soul, and we saw it taken up into heaven like a flash of lightning.

9. A certain woman, Eusebia, appropriately named because she lived piously, sought out the body of the martyr and, bedecking his holy body with wine and precious ointments, she wrapped it in a clean shroud, placed it in a casket in her house and celebrated there his commemoration to the glory of almighty God and of our Lord Jesus Christ and of the Holy Spirit. The holy martyr of Christ Theodore died on the 8th of June,[116] during the reigns of the emperors Maximianus and Maximinus, but also during the rule of our lord Jesus Christ, to whom, with the Father and the Holy Spirit, be glory and power for ever and ever, amen.

---

114 The final sentence, 'Grant also, Lord ... prize' is an addition to the account in the *Acta Polycarpi* 14.3. The sentiments are a common element in martyrdom accounts and recall Paul's encouragement to the various Christian communities to whom he wrote.

115 Cf. *Passio SS. Eutropii, Cleonici et Basilisci*; Delehaye 1909: 41–43.

116 This is in fact the date of the commemoration for Theodore the General. The confusion is indicative of the ways in which the two had become intertwined by the tenth–eleventh centuries, when the earliest extant mss were copied. One ms (cod. Bibl. Angelicae gr. 81, 12th c.) does preserve the correct date of February 17. Note Delehaye 1925a: 39.

Text 3: *BHG* 1765, ed. Sigalas 1925: 225–226; Delehaye 1925a: 45–46[117]

The life and upbringing of the holy martyr Theodore

[225] The father of St Theodore was Erythraios, a good man who loved the poor, and his mother – who was married to Erythraios as a virgin – was called Polyxene, and in the first year of their marriage the noble Theodore was born to them. When his mother died in childbirth, and his father was unable to find a Christian wet nurse, he devised a means of nourishing the infant. So, after cleaning kernels of wheat and grinding barley, he boiled them both with water as appropriate, and mixing in a sufficient amount of honey, used to put them into a glass vessel in the shape of a teat. The infant, holding this in his mouth instead of the breast, gladly sucked out the liquid just like milk. Then, as time passed and the infant's teeth developed, his father fed him through a funnel on finely flavoured wheaten bread soaked in white wine, and later on the softer fruits and most nourishing vegetables.[118] But he did not permit any meat to be given to the child as he was growing up.[119]

He placed the boy in his sixth year with a certain Proclus, a teacher of basic letters.[120] And after attending his lessons for three years he was made a soldier of Caesar[121] in the legion guarding the city of

117　Page references in square brackets in the text are to Sigalas 1925.

118　Obviously an improbable tale if a newborn is concerned, but might reflect the practice of nursing babies after their first few months, in the absence of a mother or wet-nurse: see Bourbou and Garvie-Lock 2009: 70–75, who comment, however (74), that feeding honey to infants would cause severe food poisoning. It is worth noting that attitudes to wet-nursing were ambivalent: see Lascaratos and Poulakou-Rebelakou 2003; Beaucamp 1983. On baby feeders, see also Pitarakis 2009: 215–216.

119　Avoidance of meat was a standard practice in Christian ascetic contexts: see Text 2: §1; and p. 59 n. 8 above; cf. *Vita Theod. Syk.*, §6.

120　χαμαιδιδάσκαλος – on elementary school teachers: Kalogeras 2000: 232–237. The standard educational pattern entailed the acquisition of basic reading and numeracy, beginning at the age of 6 or 7. Thereafter it was possible, for those whose families or circumstances permitted, to continue to a secondary stage to study grammar and, thereafter, rhetoric. See Kalogeras 2000: 121–142; also Moffatt 1986; Kaster 1983. For the stages of childhood: Prinzing 2009 with the literature in Pitarakis 2009: 167–168.

121　Recruitment at the age of 9 may seem unlikely, but in fact boys were regularly enrolled into their father's unit after the latter died (although technically they could not serve until they were 19 or 20 years of age), and the presence of young boys on campaign was not unusual. See Jones 1964: 615–616, 653; Elton 1996: 128–129. On the other hand, recruitment of boys who were clearly underage seems to be a middle Byzantine phenomenon and is associated with government insistence on the maintenance of fiscal obligations. The text

Amasia.[122] A certain Helladius, a Christian living in virtue and possessing the grace of God, dwelt on the sloping plain before the city, which is called Thera,[123] and where the unit of soldiers was assembled. Observing the young man progressing to the height of skill in arms, training along with his peers, thinking about warfare in peace and recognising that he possessed a soul capable of martyrdom for Christ, [226] Helladius frequently exhorted him to share in his meals. And, nourishing him with suitable counsel, he convinced him to fight not for the mortal but rather for the immortal king.

Now, since Theodore was the best among his companions both in mind and in bodily strength as well as in good will toward the commander, some of the soldiers who were envious of his virtue slandered him to the commander, saying that he detested the gods and privately worshipped a foreign deity. When he had interrogated him the commander realised that he was a Christian and was on the one hand greatly distressed, especially because he regarded him with affection, but nevertheless strongly admonished him, promising him distinctions and promotions and much money as well as the good opinion of the emperor, if only he would undertake to sacrifice willingly to Rhea and Ares. And he reminded him also of his present youthfulness and of the most terrible of punishments and that he should not violently destroy his present life.

But since the commander saw that Theodore was not in the least convinced, replying rather with more openness and confirming that he had enlisted in the service of Christ the king, the commander ordered that he be locked up in prison and be subject to beating and finally be consumed by fire.

And so the noble soldier of Christ courageously defeated impiety, and having died in the city of Amasia in Helenopontus, some gentle and

---

here may thus inadvertently reveal its later date of composition. See Haldon 1993: 26, n. 70; 32–33; cf. the example of Euthymios the Younger, enrolled at the age of 7 because his family owed military service: *Vita Euthymii iunioris*, 172.19ff.

122 Amasia was an important garrison town in Helenopontus, situated on a site of considerable natural strength overlooking the Iris river. It lay at a strategic crossroads linking Gangra and Tavium to the west with Sebasteia to the east, and then further south-eastwards via Dazimon and Dokeia to Sebasteia, thence to Satala and beyond; or eastwards to Neokaisareia (Niksar), Koloneia, Satala and Theodosioupolis (Erzerum). See Ramsay 1890: 317–330; Cumont and Cumont 1906: 2: 146–184; Foss and Winfield 1986: 17–19.

123 The beginning of the valley that eventually opens into the plain of Chiliokomon: see Strabo, *Geography* xii, 3. 39. The names were selected probably on the grounds of their 'ancient' associations. See e.g. for Helladius *RE* VIII, 1: 102–104; Proclus recalls the like-named patriarch of Constantinople (434–446) or perhaps the neoplatonic philosopher: *RE* XXIII, 1: 183–186, 186–247.

devout men wrapped up his remains and placed them piously in a tomb.[124] But the brothers dwelling in Euchaïta argued fiercely with their fellows in Amasia, wishing to take the remains of the holy man, saying that he had issued this instruction while still alive.[125] I do not know what the outcome of this rivalry was. But I have written the above for your Perfectness, so that through it other Christians might be strengthened in the name of the Lord Jesus Christ.

Text 4: *BHG* 1764, ed. Delehaye 1909: 183–201; 1925: 49–55

The life before the martyrdom and the upbringing and growing-up and the wondrous miracles of the holy and most glorious megalomartyr[126] *Theodore*

[183] 1. Praise be to God the Father of our Lord Jesus Christ who blesses us with every spiritual bounty, who brings us together annually at this time of the year in the dwelling-place[127] of the victor, in which is stored the treasure of his body, more precious than any possessions, as in the holy mount Sion, to hearken to his commands and to be guided by them – he who is now well-pleased in the wealth of his compassion that we come once more to this festival for the birthday celebration, for the praise and the glory of the power of his great might; and who has deemed us, unworthy as we are, to be ministers of divine mysteries and teachers of his miracles. Blessed be the name of his glory forever and ever more, because the whole earth has

---

124 A number of key features of Theodore's *passio* are absent from this account: the dragon episode was certainly a later (probably sixth-century) addition; but there is no mention of the pious Eusebia, nor of the burning of the temple (although the gods Rhea and Ares are mentioned).

125 It is difficult to know whether this really does indicate an early account, as argued by Sigalas 1937: 99–102 – perhaps fourth-century – or merely a later attempt to furnish appropriate details (including the name of Theodore's father and mother) to render the account more persuasive or legitimate and explain the focus of the cult being in Euchaïta rather than in Amasia. See discussion at pp. 32–34 above.

126 The epithet '*megalomartyr*', 'great martyr', was commonly applied to saints such as Theodore, Demetrius, George and others: see *Miracles of St Thekla*: 416, n. 15.

127 σκηνή. Lit. a tent, but used in hagiographical and theological contexts to refer to a habitation – in this case the church of St Theodore at Euchaïta is presumably intended – or other form of dwelling. See Lampe 1961, s.v. Delehaye noted the similarity in the wording of this opening with that in the *Life* of Theodore of Sykeon: 1909: 34.

been filled with knowledge of the Lord. So, as though awaking from the sleep of our lethargy through the aid of the all-Holy Spirit, knowing from holy scripture that everyone who commences a word and deed takes their beginning from God and is bound to return to repose in God, then let us make a beginning now.

2. Christ is our God and our peace, brethren, he who in his mercy for us rose up from his father's bosom, descended to earth and took on human flesh from the holy virgin, the [184] God-bearing Mary; who, proceeding from her, was both perfect God and perfect man, and *has broken down in his flesh the dividing wall of hostility*;[128] who was the first martyr, ascending the cross and in so doing destroying the power of the devil; who redeemed us from the power of darkness and released us into his kingdom. *He took away our lawlessness and he bore our sickness.*[129] Therefore we also beseech him, he who plucks out the sickness of the world, that we may venture to recount a few of the miracles that have come down to us of the holy and glorious great martyr Theodore, adhering to the limit and standard of the truth and embellishing the account with nothing further. For the sea no more makes entreaty of the rivers that flow into it, be they ever so many and mighty, than does he who is now lauded demand praise from those who will approach him; since while he is presented to all those who assemble as an immaterial delicacy and a nourishment higher than all mortal things, yet through prayer has it been given to us, most poor in spirit, to strive in deed and in word in order to bring the people of the Lord to imitation and emulation of his virtuous conduct and of his warm and unfeigned faith in God. Looking toward this end alone and with nothing else in mind, let us recount those things worthy of mention and pass over in silence those that are not. Therefore the upbringing and martyrdom of the most holy man should be written – whence he came, and for what reason, having come here, he loved this place and was contented in it – to cast light in advance on the miracles, so that a different generation, sons still to be born, might know and relate these things to their sons also, that they may place their hope in God and pursue with him [Theodore] the same measure of virtue.[130] Insofar as this is attainable by us, let us employ concise language; for a surfeit of words, especially when generated by an

---

128 Ephes. 2. 14.
129 A slight rewording of Matt. 8. 17: 'He took our illnesses and bore our diseases' (τὰς ἀσθενείας ἡμῶν ἔλαβεν καὶ τὰς νόσους ἐβάστασεν), following Isaiah 53. 4.
130 Cf. Ps. 102. 18–19.

incompetent and simple intellect, is the enemy of listening. On account of which I beg my readers to grant forgiveness.[131]

3. The native land of the holy and great martyr Theodore [185] was the country towards the rising sun; for he was indeed of noble birth in the east.[132] His father was named Erythrios, his mother Polyxene. But she died in childbirth, and since his father was unable to find a Christian woman for a wet-nurse, he devised a means of feeding the infant. Cleaning grains of wheat and grinding barley he boiled them both together properly in water, and mixing them with honey in proportion, he put them into a glass vessel shaped like a teat, which the infant held in his mouth instead of the breast and sucked out the liquid sweetly just like milk. As time passed and the infant's teeth developed, his father fed him on fine wheaten bread soaked in water and on the softer fruits and the most nourishing vegetables, for the saint did not deign to eat any meat as he was growing up. In his sixth year he placed the boy under a teacher of the Christians and after spending a few years with him the boy was made a soldier of the emperor, although against his will. For when his father died the noble youth was taken from his native city to a military unit, and thus came with many others to Amasia, where the winter quarters of the soldiers had been assigned by the rulers. But since Theodore surpassed all his comrades-in-arms in all respects, in strength and in size and in honesty in his behaviour and in good will towards the commander, some of his fellows, as a result of envy, slandered him to the latter, accusing him of hating the gods and of privately worshipping some foreign deity.[133] When blessed Theodore learned this, imitating his own Lord Christ, he went away for a short time, for he possessed both the preparation and the understanding that he would easily bear all those trials for which Christ crowns the martyrs. But since he also wanted his contest to be proper (since the law of martyrdom neither turns away from those who willingly seek after it nor from those who are

---

131 The anonymous author takes the tone of this introduction from the text of Chrysippos' encomium (Text 1 above) and from Gregory of Nyssa's homily, as will readily be seen by comparing the three.

132 An echo of the equivalent lines in Gregory of Nyssa: 'The fatherland of this noble man was the region where the sun rises. He was of noble birth; just like Job he was from the east, and with the latter he had not only his fatherland in common but neither did he omit the imitation of his character' (ed. Cavarnos 1990: 64. 23–25, trans. Leemans 2003: 86). For the value of 'nobility' in hagiographic contexts see Caseau 2009: 140–143.

133 Here (from 'His father was named Erythrios … ' to ' … foreign deity') the author borrows his text, with a few minor changes, from Text 3.

sickly; nor when it is at hand, does it delay – the one being presumptuous,
the other faint-hearted) and even though he respected the Lawgiver in this,
what did he contrive?[134] Or rather, towards what end [186] was he borne,
moved by the providence that wisely shows consideration from afar for all
our affairs? Secretly slipping out of Amasia, and after crossing the plain
that lay before it, he reached a lofty hill at sunset. When he reached its
summit, standing up on high he looked all around, delighted by what he
saw and rejoicing in spirit at the landscape lying serenely before him. He
spied a fine wooded grove lying below and, descending, stayed a short
while; but finding no water with which to relieve his thirst, gazing up into
the heavens above and recalling to himself the divine voice which called to
Moses, the servant of God, '*Why criest thou to me?*'[135] he offered inwardly
a prayer to the Lord of glory, saying, 'Behold Lord and ruler of all, grant
the consolation of refreshment now also to those who invoke your most
wondrous name, knowing that on account of my faith in you and your
only-begotten son and our Lord Jesus Christ I have purposefully chosen
the one all-powerful divinity and I hasten in yearning to you to be deemed
worthy of martyrdom.' And straight away, just as the psalmist says, that *the
Lord is near to all that call upon him in truth* and *he will perform the will
of them that fear him*,[136] no sooner had the martyr had these thoughts than
the Lord looked upon him and worked a wonder there, granting through
him [Theodore] an abundant spring of living water, which to this very day
affords great wonder to those who pass along that road and who encounter
it, enjoying in plenty the bounty of that God-given and never-failing spring.
Wherefore it happens that everyone praises in song the God of miracles.
For just as our God, the God of the prophets, once hearkened unto the great
Isaiah, when Jerusalem was besieged by the enemy and burned with thirst,
and he poured out that great and wondrous spring of Shiloh which, when it
had been despatched,[137] the creator was glad to have been called by name,

---

134 Cf. *Acta Polycarpi* 1. 2; and esp. 4. Christian authorities disagreed about whether
voluntary martyrdom – of which there are a number of examples reported in the sources –
was appropriate or not, with several condemning it while others approved: see Gross 2005:
1–5.

135 Exodus 14. 15.

136 Ps. 145. 118–119.

137 The pool or water of Siloam/Shiloh was an important reservoir for Jerusalem,
collecting water from the channels or aqueducts on the western side of the Kidron valley
(Mare 1992b). In the year 701 BCE, during the reign of Hezekiah, when the city was
threatened with attack by the Assyrian ruler Sennacherib, the supply was assured through
the construction of a conduit, in which a commemorative inscription has been found (Sasson

thus saving his own people, so it was also granted here to the victorious martyr.

[187] 4. Having then relieved his thirst, he was pleased to make inhabited a place formerly dry and deserted through lack of water, in a word benefiting all right up to this day. So, giving thanks for this remarkable miracle and singing hymns of praise to the generous Lord, being confident in soul and encouraged in spirit, through some divine influence the most illustrious martyr looked about and espied a high mountain opposite, with a small estate lying at its foot, far from the crowds of the city. Being delighted in it, full of beasts and *all the reptiles that creep on the earth*,[138] when he reached it and found a place that was watered and leafy and isolated, or, to put it more accurately, that was in every respect far from the insults and harm of those who betrayed him, he dismounted from the saddle and sat down quietly. And he espied a very clear, sweet spring and a great thicket standing there, in which lurked a wild beast in the form of a dragon, on account of which the place was inaccessible; for no-one, neither man nor beast, dared to approach it, for anything that came close was instantly destroyed by such a savage creature. But through the foresight of God who disposes wisely of all things, and who foresees through his love of mankind the better things and those tending towards salvation, the mistress of the above-mentioned estate unexpectedly happened to be present. She was of senatorial rank and of the imperial family, of those who wielded the scepter of the Roman state, that is to say, the relatives of Maximianus and Maximinus. Since these two knew that she was devoted to and worshipped Christ and had contempt for their idolatry, yet respected her, for she had raised them as a mother (and because of this wishing to preserve a natural filial piety), they plotted in the evil purpose of their own mind to put her aside and to send her away from her own land. But she desired this, or rather lovingly embraced the withdrawal from Rome, thus by God's design offering salvation to many souls. [188] And so, accompanied by a generous escort from them and by her own property and household, she arrived at the city of Amasia, where she chose to settle.[139] And as she was there with full permission and

---

1982; Broshi 1974); the besieging army was (probably) struck by a pestilence and forced to withdraw. The passage here presumably refers to these events. See 2 Chron. 32; 2 Kings 18. 13–19. 35; Isaiah 22. 9–11.

138 Cf. Gen. 1. 28; 30.

139 As noted already in the Introduction, while assuming any factual accuracy within such martyrdom accounts would certainly be foolhardy, historical examples sometimes underlie

authority, the citizens welcomed her with gifts, since she was of imperial blood and carried imperial orders for the current authorities, to the effect that she be granted every privilege and appropriate honours and be obeyed; and in addition that various dwellings and fertile properties be granted her tax-free to provide ease of circumstances. And all the tyrants' commands were carried out. Having welcomed her and having seen how, just like her pious name, she lived piously and how she honoured the Lord Christ, the faithful landowners turned to her eagerly and happily. Since idolatry was growing apace at that time, and many martyrs had been seized on account of their belief in Christ, the Christ-loving Eusebia, courageously and carefully taking care for the living, also visited the relics of the saints, and having anointed them reverently with sweet oils, laid them to rest on her own properties.[140] So, as we said, by divine will she happened to be present on her own estate, which was called Euchaïta. Standing and looking down she espied the saint's horse and, knowing how perilous and dangerous the place was for passers-by, she immediately despatched servants and, I believe, invited the martyr to come to her.

5. But he did not wish to obey; so standing up in fervent zeal and running forward a little in spite of herself, for she did not dare to come close to the place, stretching out her hand she cried, 'O sir, withdraw, leave that place'; and she called to him and beseeched him, beckoning with her hand [to him] not to tarry longer there but to come to her. The saint, convinced by her great insistence, did so and drawing close and perceiving her appearance and her stately manner, considered whether he might confide his situation to her. [189] The truly Christ-loving Eusebia, illumined by divine grace and understanding the martyr's God-pleasing purpose, asked him whence he had come and to what end. And so, when the saint had spoken openly and entrusted to her all the facts, and [explained] that he had withdrawn on account of his Christian faith, and when, with great joy, she had heard this,

---

the detail, as here in the case of Eusebia, whose story may well reflect events associated with certain imperial women in the fourth and fifth centuries. Note also that by the sixth century Euchaïta was well established as a place of internal banishment, in particular for churchmen, and it remained such until the later eleventh century: see pp. 13–14 above. The author of the encomium may well be drawing on the awareness among his audience of such tales or traditions.

140 See above, pp. 25–27: again, perhaps reminiscent of the activities of Eudocia (*PLRE* 2:408–409), the wife of Theodosius II, and possibly recalling also the progress of the empress Helena in the Holy Land: Lenski 2004: 114–115 and esp. 119–120.

she made the sign of the cross on her forehead and said to the martyr, 'My lord, I too am a Christian who despises the disgusting sacrificial stench of the idols, and I own this worthless property as my own, to do with as I wish.' And she counselled and advised him to join her, since none of the pagans had ever dared to harass her or to seize by force any of those who had taken refuge with her, since she enjoyed the full protection and favour of those who ruled the Roman empire at that time, the tyrants Maximianus and Maximinus.[141] But when the true martyr of Christ heard these words, speaking boldly in the Lord, he said to her, 'I beg you, mistress and spiritual mother, permit me to depart and fulfill my purpose ordained by God. For I would choose rather to be swallowed up by this dragon than to bow down before the false dumb idols and to worship creation rather than the creator. I believe in our Lord Jesus Christ the only-begotten son of God, our true God, and that through his mighty power I will pierce and destroy the dragon that used to lurk in this thicket. And thus I will journey on, confident that I will conquer our enemy the devil who works through the sons of disobedience of these idolatrous men.' Hearing these words and raising up her hands, she besought God, the ruler of all, He who holds all things in his hands, to fight alongside him [Theodore], that he might complete his contest on His behalf. When the saint stood his ground there steadfastly and courageously, the fearsome dragon slithered towards him, and the mighty martyr pierced it with his spear [190] and killed it. And he sent up hymns of thanks to the master of all things, our Lord Jesus Christ, for he had freed that place from the designs of such a savage creature, so that thereafter and to this day all can pass by without fear and after enjoying that most sweet and everlasting spring, glorify the all-powerful Lord.

6. Thereupon, when the aptly-named and Christ-loving Eusebia saw the invincible martyr entirely unharmed and the fearful beast lying utterly vanquished at his feet, she glorified the marvellous name of our Saviour God, and thus the holy woman offered the appropriate thanks to the martyr. And he said to her, 'Spiritual mother, since by divine will Christ saw fit that I should come here and slay this real dragon through the weapon of the precious cross, I believe in our one and only immortal God, who loves mankind, that by the grace of my Christ I will also trample upon

---

141 One wonders whether the emphasis placed on this imperial protection and freedom from harassment reflects generally understood or known facts about such high-ranking exiles in Euchaïta and elsewhere at the time the *passio* was written.

the head of the spiritual dragon. Wherefore I deem your holiness worthy not to disregard my request, but that you be present in the aforementioned city and when, with His help, I complete the journey of my promise to Him, that you carry off this, my humble corpse, to this place and lay it to rest here, where through the power of my Christ I slew this dragon. For it is here that my soul desires and I have chosen that my death and departure from life occur on this estate of yours, for the eternal repose and commemoration of your Christ-loving soul. And I will beseech the judge, my Christ, on account of His good will towards me, to bestow upon you a worthy reward on the day of His appearance in the eternal light of His father's glory.' Hearkening to these words, and convinced by the victorious martyr's many oaths, she agreed with him to do all that he commanded, trusting through him in the Lord of glory, and promoting him as a martyr for the truth; and for these reasons [191] she received the victorious and greatly beloved martyr into her house, he who had worked there three miracles. These were driving out the wild creatures and snakes that dwelt on the estate, simply through tearful prayers to God;[142] slaying, by means of the panoply of the precious cross of Christ, the dragon that lurked in the thicket by the water and that slaughtered all who came near; and through his granting refreshment from the most clear and sweet spring to those who approached. So the holy Eusebia, seeing all these things and recognising the man's holiness even before his martyrdom, fell to her knees before him, begged him to pray for her and for that place, and to give no thought to these passing and uncertain earthly human values nor this fleeting life, but to reap the reward intended by a generous God, His ineffable and incomparable kingdom of heaven, and through it enjoyment of never-ending and eternal blessings.

7. Reinforced in soul and in body by these encouraging words, the holy martyr surrendered himself entirely to God, and fortified in spirit in his faith in Him, he reached Amasia and with courageous purpose mingled with the contestants and, waiting for a quiet time of night, he set fire to the goddess Artemis, greatly honoured by the idolaters, and utterly destroyed it.[143] Thereupon, having been seized by some of the abominable guardians

---

142 Although this miracle is not included in the present text, the writer was presumably familiar with it from the encomium of Chrysippos.

143 Artemis was worshipped at Ephesus as a mother goddess, although this aspect of her divinity seems to have been limited to Ionia. Later commentators, especially Christian writers, sometimes conflated her with Cybele, as seems to be the case here. General

of the temple and brought before the governor, they loudly testified against him, that he was the one who had dared to carry out the deed and that he was the destroyer of the mother of their Gods. The tyrant, realising that he was a Christian and bore the sign of the cross and that he confessed himself, just as before, to be a servant of Christ and not of Caesar, was deeply upset, remembering his earlier goodwill towards him, [192] sternly warning him and promising once again promotions and great wealth and the honours bestowed by Caesar, if only he would undertake to sacrifice to Rhea and Ares. But his argument completely failed to move the pious martyr. When he determined that the saint remained absolutely unpersuaded, he commanded him to be imprisoned without food or drink, ordered him to be subjected to a great many beatings, had him nailed to the cross[144] and the flesh completely torn away from his ribs, and finally decreed that he should be consumed by fire, just as he had destroyed the temple of the mother of their unholy gods by fire. And so the noble warrior of Christ, suffering according to Christ's law, conquered impiety, meeting his end in the city of Amasia before the thirteenth Kalends of March[145] under the impious emperors Maximianus and Maximinus. The blessed, indeed queenly Eusebia, who was present at his martyrdom, hastening to carry out everything that had been commanded, and presenting numerous gifts to the governor, requested the precious corpse of the saint and most glorious martyr. Taking it and anointing it respectfully and treating it as both holy and hallowing those who honoured it, she carried it, together with God-fearing men, and placed it in her house, just as the saint had enjoined her. Erecting a beautiful and most august church for him, she preserved there as a treasure his most precious and blessed body. And, venerating it, she prayed in supplication to the merciful Lord night and day, that when she had died, she be laid to rest near him in blessed fashion, preserving to the end her steadfast and unshaken faith in him as guardian and protector of all her family. And indeed, this came to

---

discussion: LiDonnici 1992. The riot of metalsmiths against Paul's preaching at Ephesus, described in Acts 19. 28, a text well known and used by Christian apologists, may additionally have contributed to this tradition. For the destruction of the temple of Cybele, see above, pp. 24 and 61.

144 The author passes over the refusal of the martyr to be nailed to the cross and his steadfastness as he is prepared for the pyre, a key feature of Text 1 (Chrysippos' account), and of that in Text 2 above, borrowed from the *Acta Polycarpi.*

145 The Kalends of March = 1st of the month, thus the thirteenth day before the Kalends = 17 February.

pass, for the Lord hearkens to the prayers of the righteous, because the benevolent attitude of fellow-believers is transferred to the Lord Christ whom they have served. And he who honours those who suffered for the true faith clearly possesses an equivalent zeal [193] for the faith, whence those who are accustomed also to honour the holy martyrs likewise share jointly all the martyrs' crowns laid up in store for them. So, when the blessed and devout Eusebia died, her kin and those servants of the martyr whom she had appointed to the task piously placed her in Christ near to the saint's resting place, celebrating a memorial service for her, which we now vow to undertake forever, in return for this unblemished treasure that she granted us, on the Saturday of the mid-Lenten week,[146] just as the birthday feast of the saint is customarily celebrated throughout the world on the Saturday of the first week.

8. O victorious lord and faithful martyr for the munificent Christ, chosen provider for us and ours! We most lowly servants, tardy successors and base offshoots of your branches, our fathers and teachers, and together with us this, your worthless human flock and most humble and menial people, blessed and thrice-blessed martyr, we beseech you on our knees, since you possess God-given access to our common Lord and Saviour Christ and have undertaken the burden of caring for us. Gather together those who have been scattered and bring back those who have been carried off into captivity on account of our many transgressions by these accursed Hagarenes, who have turned away from that compassionate submission to the dispensation of our common Lord and God, on our behalf and that of all nature.[147] And lastly console those who are abandoned and do not forsake their families, but stand by and protect and watch over and lead them to the better things to come from salvation. Of those who come running and hastening earnestly and in yearning to this, the blessed hall of your holy

146 John Mauropous composed an encomium to Eusebia for her feast-day: ed. de Lagarde 1882: 202–207 (*BHG* 632), although he notes that 'we know nothing certain about her'.

147 The final prayer places emphasis on one of Theodore's key attributes, redeeming or rescuing those who have, through one cause or another, been taken away from their homes. Reference to the Hagarenes, a term not usually employed before the seventh-century Islamic conquests, may suggest that at origin this is part of an original, seventh-century prologue or version of the martyrdom, although it is quite clear that the details of the *passio* itself, esp. those relating to Eusebia, put it in the later ninth or more probably the tenth century at the earliest. In the later eleventh century, of course, the Hagarenes would be understood as the Türkmen and Selcuk raiders who plagued the central and eastern provinces of the empire from the 1040s.

tabernacle,[148] accept their prayers to God favourably and lead them on to Him and hold each of them worthy of His grace, so that we may gain through you in the midst of these earthly and transient cares the suitable and appropriate and endless [194] bounties in Christ Jesus our Lord, to whom be the glory and the power for ever and ever, amen.

Now we will do well to take up once more those matters already mentioned, so let us now commemorate in our modest account the martyr's various and greatest wonders, in proportion to the glory of God, just as we promised. For if we wished to relate all such things as we have been deemed worthy to have heard and to have seen, the short time allotted us would be insufficient for the telling.[149]

[Miracle 1]
While she remained alive the devout and martyr-loving Eusebia continued to be assiduous in her veneration of the remains of the saint, and she wanted to have an image of him painted for her to keep. But when she came to one of the painters and explained the saint's form and features, she was unable to fulfill her desire through his hand, and so she returned home in great despondency. But not very long after this, the saint arrived in the guise of a soldier returning from a long journey and commanded the painter to tell him what the woman had ordered. And when he had told him, the martyr said to him, 'Paint me just as you see me, and it will certainly please her.' And so, when the image was painted and the saint had vanished, well, she came once more, and learning of the saint's appearance, raising her eyes and her hands on high, she sang heartfelt praise to God, who had by this act fulfilled her heart's desire. Taking the image, she returned in joy to her home at Euchaïta. And the image is preserved by the grace of Christ to this day. Thus are the saints well pleased with those who love them and, when they are so minded, grant their requests.[150]

---

148 As noted in the Introduction, such references here and in the opening paragraphs of Text 4 make the location and occasion of the reading of the encomium and the miracle stories quite clear.

149 While these final words leading into the miracles themselves are fairly standard and typical of such accounts, they are also particularly reminiscent of the sentiments expressed at the end of Chrysippos' encomium.

150 Since this miracle is clearly very different in tone and theme from those that follow, it raises the question of whether it was part of the original collection or perhaps a later addition. In the encomium of Nikephoros Ouranos, for example, it is added at the end of the martyrdom account but before the miracle of the κόλυβα (kolyva). A later addition may seem more likely, therefore, since, as noted already (above, p. 53), it was a feature of tenth- and

[Miracle 2]

In days long ago, when the godless race of the Persians had taken possession of our land,[151] the barbarians came to Euchaïta and searched high and low in the holy shrine of the saint[152] for his [195] precious relics, not in the desire for prayer (for they worshipped fire and water, venerating what was created rather than the creator), their wits being deceived by a demonic power. But when the revered bones of the saint were revealed, they filled the Persians with a great fragrance, so that many of those present who were possessed by unclean spirits were freed, and a great many suffering from diverse illnesses and bodily ailments were healed. And, recognising the wonder-working power accorded the relics by our lord Jesus Christ, each of those who had been healed by faith stored some of them away for himself as though they were protective medicines. But not long thereafter they had unwillingly to give everything back, for the martyr brought it about that his own honoured body, undivided and unsullied, should be kept in the very same hallowed enclosure which he had chosen. For God never ceased to look out for our city, so that the city quaked and trembled until the heaps of earth with the bones were made visible to all. The barbarians, astonished at these events, turned to fear and panic – for even the foe knows to marvel at the great deeds of God – and they permitted the relics that had been divided up among them to be returned to the Christians who had gathered, without omitting anything at all. Indeed, collecting everything together without exception and placing

---

eleventh-century hagiography that saints were concerned with their appearance in imagery, and there are several other examples to underline the point. John Mauropous refers to an image of the saint 'on foot' in the third of his eulogies on Theodore the recruit, an image that is attributed with miraculous properties (ed. de Lagarde 1882: 207–209), and this particular miracle story may relate to (or the writer may have wished to encourage the listeners to make this connection to) the same image.

151 The war with the Persians under Khusru II Parviz broke out in 602 and lasted until Heraclius' final victory in the late 620s.

152 The location of the church of St Theodore is discussed in detail by Trombley 1985: 67, who argues for its being outside the Anastasian wall (in miracle 2 the Persians are able to enter the shrine, while in miracle 3 they are clearly stated to have been encamped outside or before the city). The survey of the lower village between 2006 and 2010 located (in Area 3) what appears to be a cruciform basilican structure associated with a range of architectural and decorative fragments suggesting a church, in turn surrounded by as-yet-unexplored structures, possibly associated with this building. Super-intensive survey rendered this identification very probable, and this may indeed be the church described in the miracles and referred to in other texts discussed above in the Introduction. See Bikoulis et al. 2015; Haldon and Elton 2007: 3 and fig. 9b; Haldon et al. 2009: 5–6.

them in a clean shroud, these sinners left an old man from among the captives to look after them, so that they could be handed over to the then bishop of our city, the great Eleutherios (he who afterwards rebuilt this holy church),[153] and they left the city. And when this had been completed Eleutherios deposited the remains of the Victor – honoured and revered by us beyond any gold and silver – in their own special place by the saint's resting place, to the glory and honour of the martyr's greatness.[154] But let us return to the matter at hand.

[Miracle 3]

While the Persians were still before the city, [196] they were suddenly attacked by a Roman force[155] and, boiling over in great rage, they put many of the captives to the sword and burned down the whole city and the shrine of the saint. But they were not quite able to escape, since the warrior martyr caught them. For not very far along the road another body of Roman troops attacked them again and killed many of them near the mountain known as Omphalimos. But God's justice destroyed the survivors, who got as far as the Lykos river,[156] by showering down hail as big as stone missiles from the

153 Although some seventh-century bishops of Euchaïta are known from their lead seals or their signatures to the acts of the councils of 680 and 692, Eleutherios is otherwise unattested. See the Introduction, above, pp. 12 and 16.

154 Assuming that this account was intended for a local congregation or audience – at least when it was first composed – who would certainly have known whether or not it was accurate, the text makes it plain that the saint's remains were still, in the period between 615 and the later 620s, kept in his church at Euchaïta.

155 Trombley 1985: 68 suggests either 615 or 624 as possible dates for this Persian attack and Roman counter-attack, and links the tactics employed to those described in the *Strategikon* of Maurice for flanking manoeuvres (*ibid.* 72–74). Zuckerman 1988: 206–210 connects this Roman attack with the activities of imperial forces during Heraclius' first Persian campaign in 622, and although quite plausible, one wonders why the emperor Heraclius himself, who commanded this thrust, does not receive a mention in our text. Howard-Johnston 1995: 134 n. 11 proposes instead 624/625, during Heraclius' preparations and campaigning before the great siege of Constantinople in 626, and associates the account in the miracle with the defeat in this region of the Persians under Šahin by Heraclius' brother Theodore, raising also the possibility that the hagiographical account plays specifically on the name Theodore in this context.

156 Mount Omphalimos is most probably the Mt Ophlimos referred to by Strabo in eastern Helenopontus (*Geography* xii, 3. 30), which can be located south of the modern settlements of Taşsove, Erbaa and Gözpınar: see Talbert 2000: 87/4B (36.13–36.44 E/40.40–40.20 N). See also Zuckerman 1988: 207–208. The Lykos (modern Kelkit Çayı) is the longest tributary of the Iris (mod. Yeşilırmak), which it joins at mod. Kızılçubuk, close to ancient Eupatoria. The route followed by the Persian force on its retreat must have been along the road from

heavens, so that not one perpetrator of those evil deeds returned home. The Roman army, in thanks to the martyr, built from the foundations up on that very spot a shrine in the name of the martyr who had been the cause of the victory and whom they, as they swore, considered to be their champion and fellow-warrior. And the shrine stands to this day.[157]

[Miracle 4]
In the fourteenth year of the God-guarded and Christ-loving reign of Constantine, when the peace between Romans and Saracens was over, at the beginning of the seventh indiction, the accursed Hagarenes invaded and devastated all our land on account of our sins.[158] For truly, the evils that fall upon those who are attacked are a just judgment of God on those who deserve punishment. For, as the prophet Hosea says, 'War descended upon the children of disobedience and nations shall be against them to chastise them in their iniquity.'[159] So, when they were present in our land and were at last approaching our city, a most holy woman, who had had a vision, announced it to many people, saying that she had seen a great throng of barbarians standing before the walls of our city. As they wanted to enter through the gate,[160] she beheld the martyr quite clearly, armed and mounted

---

Euchaïta eastwards to Amasia and then north-east along the road that runs beside the Iris/ Yeşilırmak as far as the old Roman bridge across the latter, before turning south-east to the point at which the Lykos/Kelkit flows into the Iris, perhaps with the intention of marching down by way of Neokaisareia/Niksar to Comana Pontica (some seven miles from mod. Tokat). There is a much more difficult route south-eastwards from Amasia along the Iris and then eastwards towards Dokeia and Dazimon, a route which also eventually meets the Lykos, but on the face of it this seems a less likely option if the Persian forces wanted a rapid retreat eastwards. The hailstorm presumably struck them at the point at which they had reached the confluence of the Lykos and Iris rivers. For routes around Euchaïta and Amasia, see Bryer and Winfield 1985: 12ff.

157 On such shrines see comments, with further examples, in Trombley 1985: 68.

158 Discussion of the chronological information given here and the peace between Constans II and Mu'āwiya, broken by the latter in 659: above, [40–41]; and esp. Artun 2008.

159 See Hosea 4–5 and 10. 9–10.

160 No visible remains of the gate were observed during the 2006–2010 survey. The main road into the city is referred to in the encomium of Gregory of Nyssa, but the topographical and archaeological evidence suggests that this was probably not the present-day road leading south-east from modern Beyözü to Mecitözü and the modern west–east highway. The latter was constructed in the 1970s and runs parallel to and north of the old Roman and later Ottoman road (see Craft forthcoming). Rather, the connecting road probably followed the track from the south-west, past a series of Roman tombs, to reach the lower town, where the corner of a substantial wall footing can be seen within the modern road surface. The Anastasian inscription was reported by local residents to have been taken from this area,

and positioned in the centre of the gateway [197] and nobly fighting them off. She saw this at the spot where of old the martyr worked his wonder above the gate against the savage Scyths and Huns.[161] For as often as the Hagarenes threw themselves forward, as often did he hurl them back again – for they were quite unable to withstand the cross and the martyr for Christ – until at last she saw some angelic power on high and heard this voice, saying to him, 'Let them pass through the entrance, for they have not come to make war on the land without the Lord's assent.' Upon hearing these words, so the woman recounted, the saint straight away withdrew, handing the entrance over to them without resistance, yet inwardly entreating the Divinity with these words: '*Deliver not to the wild beasts a soul that gives praise to thee*, O Lord Christ our God. *Look upon your covenant now* and recall my body that was burned for you. Have mercy upon your people, beside whom you have deemed me worthy to stand, and let not these foes utterly defile the dwelling of this your servant.'[162] And when then as always the martyr had cried out these words, the sole lover of mankind, He who by nature possesses goodness, accepted his entreaties and took pity on us sinners. *He has not dealt with us according to our sins, nor recompensed us according to our iniquities, for as the heaven is high above the earth, the Lord has [so] increased his mercy toward us*, in that he is merciful, patient, most compassionate and forgives us our evil deeds.[163] For truly, the punishment was for us an act of clemency, since by chastising justly, he instructed us, yet did not abandon us to the death of despair.[164] And so, by the grace of the holy spirit, we all came safely to the stronghold[165] save but a few.

---

near the proposed line of the city walls (based on a series of features associated with such a structure: see Haldon et al. forthcoming and 2010).

161 Reference to Theodore's saving the city from the Gothic threat in 379–380, and again from the Huns in the reign of Anastasius. See above, p. 55. For representations of Theodore and other saints saving cities or standing guard at the gates: Walter 1999: 175–176.

162 See Ps. 74. 18–19.

163 Ps. 103. 10–11.

164 Cf. Joel 2. 13; 18.

165 ἐν τοῖς ὀχυρώμασι. For the term τὰ ὀχυρώματα, see Dagron and Mihaescu 1986: 225–230; note that in miracle 9, below, the same location is described as 'the *kastron*' (Delehaye 1909: 200. 5). For the defences of the acropolis at Euchaïta, see the helpful discussion in Trombley 1985: 68–70, some of whose conclusions were borne out by the 2006–2010 survey. This showed, first, that the line of the lower city wall (that built or repaired under Anastasius, see above, pp. 14–15) ran across the southern edge of the settlement between two outlying spurs of the Avkat Dağı. The much higher spur behind and to the north-east of the city, from which a track leads up from the north-eastern corner

You see, lovers of Christ, the kind of access to God that the saints possess, and how they always bring to him their intercessions on our behalf. So let us revere the honoured relics of the great holy martyr [198] deemed worthy to reside among us, and so let us celebrate as a privilege the annual memorial of his illustrious courage. For we know that although he too was but a man, yet since he suffered most nobly and endangered himself gladly for the sake of his reverence for Christ, we crown him with appropriate honours, allotting him the highest rank for the brilliance of his courageous achievements, to the glory of Christ the sole good God and our saviour.

[Miracle 6][166]
At that time, when that hateful race of enemies filled our city and were spending the winter there,[167] their leader happened to be moved by some demonic malice, and he ordered a number of picks and levers to be used against the most beautiful and pleasing shrine of the saint, with the intention of destroying it utterly as far as its foundations.[168] So he summoned all his men into the said honoured shrine and explained to them his evil plan concerning it. But while the words were still in his mouth, God's anger rose up against him and he fell headlong to the ground, rolling about, foaming at the mouth and chewing his tongue. The barbarians, snatching him up,

---

of the lower settlement (the modern access road is tractor-built and cuts a path around the eastern/south-eastern side of the promontory itself), was defended by a substantial wall with bastions and a heavily fortified gateway on its northern and more easily approached aspect, while traces of a now heavily eroded circuit wall defending the steep and in places cliff-like south-western and south-eastern sides were identified. This, then, was the acropolis or *ochyrōmata* to which the population could retire in times of stress. A large number of structures within this fortified area were identified through remote-sensing (GPR and magnetometry), although not yet excavated or otherwise investigated archaeologically, while the surface ceramics consisted of substantial quantities of late Roman or early–middle Byzantine roof tiles and some coarse wares. See Haldon and Elton 2007: figs 7a–7c, 8a–8c, 11; Watters and Wilkes 2007: 43–62 (geophysical survey results and provisional interpretation); Haldon et al. forthcoming.

166 This is the fifth miracle in the collection, but numbered 6 in the ms: see discussion above, p. 50.

167 Arab forces began to overwinter on Byzantine territory from the early 660s onwards, although there may be occasions before this not mentioned by the sources. See above (pp. 51–52) with literature.

168 They were presumably looking for plunder, but note that there is no reference here to the saint's tomb or his body, as in miracle 2 above. In light of the absence of any reference after this to the relics, it was perhaps at some point between the Persian attacks and the first Arab wintering raids that the relics were moved. See discussion above, pp. 11–12.

laid him to rest in his own lodging; and while in this way he was cut short in his satanic undertaking, yet he was not released from the hostile spirit that opposed him.

[Miracle 7][169]

Now, as we have said, after they spent the winter here and gathered together many captives from various provinces, both men and beasts, and many dead animals that had perished from cold and hunger were left lying about in the public spaces and streets and houses,[170] the whole city stank, and after a while became unbearable to the enemy. Whence they withdrew, albeit unwillingly, in the month of March. And many of the inhabitants came down from the fortifications after the enemy had left, but when they beheld the stench and desolation of the city they wished to move away from their home to other cities. But the martyr entreated God and did not permit this to take place.[171] [199] For in response to his prayers, of a sudden storm clouds moved in, and such a violent rainstorm was unleashed over this city alone such as they say had never happened in our day. And being cleansed through this storm, the city welcomed back its rejoicing inhabitants.

Behold, beloved ones, what wonders were bestowed by the most glorious martyr upon the citizens, interceding to repopulate again through the heavenly cleansing waters a city that seemed destined to become entirely uninhabited. Therefore we must now revere him through our unending devotion and festivals, he who possesses such valuable and ready access to God that not only has he rescued us from many dangers, but on many occasions from death itself through his prayers on our behalf to God, who loves mankind. For through his inexpressible compassion he heeds our genuine trust in him, nobly bearing entreaties on our behalf and granting to us unworthy souls the rich gifts he brings. Wherefore we are indebted to him for our lives, for he has saved us through his own blood.

---

169 Numbered 7 in the ms, but the sixth in the collection.

170 The topographical details given here supply valuable information both about the specific character of Euchaïta itself as well as about the type of middling urban–rural provincial settlement it represented. For a discussion and evaluation of this information, see Trombley 1985: 69–72; and the literature cited in the following note.

171 There are several examples of urban populations simply abandoning their settlement for a safer site. The information provided in this text has meant that Euchaïta has often been cited in the context of the wider debate about the fate of urban settlements during the seventh–ninth centuries: see the surveys in Brubaker and Haldon 2011: 531–548; Brandes 1989: 82–131.

[Miracle 9][172]

Understanding the insatiable desire of you faithful to hear of the wonders performed by the saints, wonders that fill the listener with joy, let us now also add this next tale to the foregoing. Because of the yearly attack of the enemy we were all staying close to the stronghold.[173] At that time one priest with a few clerics was left by the bishop in the city in order to maintain the services in the revered shrine of the saint.[174] On the eve of the spring commemoration of this glorious martyr, on the Friday of the spring service itself, the Saracens, like an unexpected storm, suddenly attacked those who were singing the thrice-holy evening hymns.[175] By the grace of Christ, so to say, they all took to flight and escaped their hands and were saved, the priest alone, who stood inside in the sanctuary, [200] being taken. Seizing him and taking him out of the city they tortured him and threatened him with death unless he betrayed those who had fled along with the holy vessels. After he had spent a sleepless night, a woman among his fellow-prisoners made a request to the priest that she might place her son, who was in the fortress, in his charge, to be cared for as his own son. For she said that in a short while the priest would be saved, and she swore that she had seen the holy martyr appear at that moment, and in a great rage against them violently snatch the priest from the clutches of the barbarians. And making her plea she absolutely insisted on her story. When morning came the barbarians, encamped before the walls, arose and handed him over to four Saracens and sent them into the city, commanding that he should either hand over those who were hiding along with the holy vessels or lose his life to the sword. But when they had entered, with him

---

172 The seventh in the collection but numbered 9 in the ms.

173 An indication of the social and economic impact of the regular raids mounted from northern Syria and northern Iraq into Anatolia in the period ca. 663–743.

174 'In the city' seems to mean the areas both within and outside of the Anastasian wall. Maintaining the regular liturgical calendar and most importantly maintaining an ecclesiastical presence in the provinces became a major issue for the church during this period. The abandonment by the clergy of exposed regions, along with the failure of some provincial bishops adequately to oversee their flocks, were severely condemned at the so-called Quinisext council of 691–692. See Quinisext canons 8 and 18 (Nedungatt and Featherstone 1995); and, for the problems faced by the clergy in such a war-torn situation, Jankowiak 2013.

175 This was most probably quite a small raiding party sent off from a larger invading column in the region, and illustrates the sort of fast raid that contributed so much to the economic and social dislocation and general insecurity of the provinces across the whole period from the 660s into the 740s.

bound and placed between them, and reached the so-called *Tetrapylon*[176] (a most suitable place for an escape!), his bonds were suddenly loosed, he thrust aside his captors as if they were cripples, and fled to safety.[177] The barbarians searched everywhere for him but, having failed to discover his whereabouts, left in shame and without success, and reported what had happened to those who had sent them. When the people of the city returned, that Saturday being the annual commemoration, the liturgy was performed in the martyr's holy shrine for God, who had rescued them so miraculously, by those who had been saved. And just as then, so we will never cease to give thanks for evermore; for as we may see, great is the power of the saints through Him. For those who lived according to God's law shall live forever, even though they depart this life; and having great access to Him they will always save those who trust in them. And that this is indeed true, hear [201] another of his miracles, no less impressive than the foregoing.

[Miracle 10][178]

On that very same Saturday, the servants of the church who had been rescued from the hands of the enemy, as we said, coming into the saint's holy shrine in order to conduct the service, found an ox tied to the railing around the martyr's tomb. They were quite at a loss to explain this, but on the next day some of those who were nearby, and had seen what happened from the adjoining hill above the city,[179] related the following. A man from

---

176 The *tetrapylon* was a monumental four-sided archway, generally placed across a major urban crossroads with each of the four entrances or passages supported by pillars or similar structures. A *tetrapylon* could be built as a single structure or as a group of separate structures. It could also function as a type of triumphal arch or simply as a decorative ornamental architectural feature. *Tetrapyla* were found throughout the Roman world and many survive, among which the best-known in the eastern parts of the empire are those at Palmyra, Gerasa and Aphrodisias. See *ODB* 1: 152; Trombley 1985: 70 and n. 36.

177 'A most suitable place for an escape' presumably because of the major streets and smaller paths that radiated out from this central place. Trombley 1985: 71 suggests that it was close to the *ochyrōmata*, but if it were, this is because the ancient and early medieval settlement within the walls was in fact quite small, covering an approximate area of some 250 × 270 m. In the context of the small and probably somewhat crowded built environment of seventh-century Euchaïta, eluding the four Saracen captors would probably not have been so difficult for someone who knew the town well and was still physically active.

178 The eighth miracle in the collection, numbered 10 in the ms.

179 The hill (or 'mountain' – the Greek term is *oros*), described further on as the ridge, clearly means the high spur on which was located the fortified area within the *ochyrōmata*.

the region of Paphlagonia[180] was bringing this ox as an offering to the saint and spent the Friday night with them. The next morning they sent him off with the ox, but having then learned of the enemy attack, they had taken to flight. From the ridge they saw the gift-bearing fellow coming back up again and, calling to him, they asked him how he managed to save himself and get back up. But he swore that he had seen nobody at all, saying 'when I went into the city and found no-one, I took the ox I had brought with me, tied it to the railing by the saint's tomb, and left.'[181] When they heard these words and saw the man safe and sound, of course they could not disbelieve him, yet they were astonished and at a loss as to how he could have passed along the same road as the enemy and escaped them. God is indeed wonderful in his saints. For just as the Assyrians who once stood by Elisha were afflicted with a hazy sight, delivered up to him as a plaything and unable to see, even though they were so close to what they sought, so now the martyr saved the man who came to him in trust, delivering him from the murderous right hand of the enemy,[182] in glory and in gratitude to Christ our God, together with glory, power, honour and reverence to God the father with the all-holy and blessed and life-giving spirit, now and forever until the end of time, Amen.

---

180 Paphlagonia lies to the west of Helenopontus, and Euchaïta is very close to the boundary between the two provinces, as reference to the map in Belke 1996 will show.

181 Cf. miracle 10 in the Chrysippos collection about the man bringing an ox as an offering to St Theodore. Note that canon 88 of the Quinisext council, repeating canon 74 of the council of 680–681, forbids bringing animals into the church except in situations of great necessity: 'No-one is to bring any beast whatsoever inside a sacred house, unless he is on a journey and, pressed by the greatest necessity, can find no house or shelter: then he shall stay in the church .... But if anyone is found bringing a beast, as has been said, into a church without necessity, if he is a cleric, he shall be deposed, if a layman, excommunicated': trans. Nedungatt and Featherstone 1995: 168–169. The case described here could be understood as one of necessity, although it is also clear that ecclesiastical discipline, especially in the provinces, must always have been difficult to maintain rigorously.

182 Cf. 2 Kings 6. 18; and cf. miracle 8 of the Chrysippos collection.

Text 5: *BHG* 1752, ed. Delehaye 1909: 168–182

This metaphrastic version follows broadly that of Niketas Paphlagon, although with a greater element of dramatic dialogue between emperor and martyr. Unlike most of the manuscripts that include this text, however, the twelfth-century manuscript that Delehaye took for his edition (Vat. gr. 1245) omits the miracle of Theodore and the dragon. Whether this was true to the original form of the Metaphrast's version or a deliberate copyist's change remains unknown.[183] Most of the elements of the interrogation and torture of the martyr are found in the passions of Theodore the Recruit and other earlier martyrs, including St Sebastian, as will readily be seen.

The martyrdom of the holy and glorious megalomartyr of Christ Theodore the General
[168] 1. A great frenzy against the true faith possessed the emperor Licinius,[184] who was subject to much idolatrous superstition. For at the first attempt he drew not a few of his subjects to his wishes and his beliefs, since these men were unsound and easily fooled, and he became furious if not all men would be prepared to believe as he did.

2. And so letters were sent out everywhere, ordering on the one hand the denial of God the creator, and on the other hand to offer sacrifice to demons and idols, and for those created by the hand of God and being his most esteemed and most fitting invention, to treat like gods the works of human hands. Therefore gifts and honors and other such services awaited those who were persuaded, whereas confiscations, threats, tortures and the final evil, death, awaited those who were not persuaded and who confessed an unchangeable faith in Christ. So this wicked order came to the ears of the great martyr Theodore, a man noble in deed, distinguished by birth and illustrious in rank – for at that time he held a general's command, which he had had obtained as a reward for his many victories. And he was spoken of [169] and loved by all; Theodore was a beloved byword for everyone.

---

183 Delehaye 1909: 31–32, who notes that in Vat. gr. 1245 the story of the dragon appears to have been begun but then deleted. In two other mss that include martyrdoms of both the saints Theodore, the dragon story is omitted from one or another of the saints' martyrdoms, raising the likelihood that copyists excluded the story deliberately where to include it would involve a repetition. On the mss: Delehaye 1909: 125–126.
184 *Augustus* 308–324.

3. And so, when he heard this command, being a Christian by family tradition, he could not bear to keep his Christian faith hidden, but speaking zealously against this impiety, he both desired to display openly his piety and did not wish thus merely to proceed to his confession [i.e. become a confessor for the faith], unless God's will consented to it.[185]

4. And so, rejoicing, he went to Heraclea Pontica,[186] for it was there, in fact, that he held a command and had been entrusted with its governorship. But the reputation of the saint did not go unnoticed by Licinius himself, and since he heard many things from many people about the holy man, he marvelled at him. So he sent a letter of friendship to summon the saint. When Theodore had read the letter, he received the messengers hospitably, and offered them hospitality for three days, refreshing them as was appropriate since they were tired on account of the journey. But he did not deem it necessary to return to the emperor, since he longed to honour his motherland and not some other place with his martyrdom, and also, indeed, to dispose properly of his affairs. And so for these reasons he dismissed them, but straight away explained most carefully in a letter the postponement of his arrival. And the letter was as follows:

5. 'The general Theodore, to the victorious emperor Licinius.[187] Your highness decided, O emperor, that I should come to Nicomedia,[188] so that I may meet with your majesty about some public or private matters, and you may make advantageous decisions about these affairs. And indeed this is worthy of imperial wisdom, thinking to explain things to one's subjects, lest in doing the opposite of those actions of which the imperial judgement approves, they might seem to err – those whom both the laws and the natural good wish to persuade to be obedient to authority. Whence,

185 In the pre-metaphrastic versions of the text, and in most later manuscripts that include this version, the miracle of Theodore and the dragon is placed here. As Delehaye notes (1909: 32), it is no longer possible to say whether the Metaphrast's own redaction of the text included or omitted this miracle.

186 Modern Ereğli: see Hoepfner 1966.

187 A very informal mode of address, possibly an attempt to echo the official address used for an emperor, but styled here to emphasise Theodore's status and also his independence of the emperor: see Rösch 1978: 142–156. The formal address to an emperor generally used the term τροπαιοῦχος rather than τροπαιοφόρος.

188 Nicomedia: mod. Izmit, and the focus for Diocletian's persecution of Christians. Galerius issued an edict of toleration there in 311, although again not observed for long. See Ruge 1936: 476–477.

after making known to your highness through bold word and deed what previously seemed to me to be well, I will then once again carry out your command, if it seems right; yet in the meantime, I do not think your ordering my visit to be expedient, as other affairs are dragging out here, and have not permitted travel elsewhere, and it will impede me with respect to my administrative duties. If indeed, therefore, your highness would rather be willing not to overlook the supplication of prudent servants, come here to Heraclea to order matters; since, O best of emperors, many of the affairs here need your supervision and concern, all of which will be well because of your highness' visit.' When the emperor had read this letter, and since he held the man in esteem and admiration, he did not reject the request, but rather was persuaded to go to Heraclea in order to visit both the saint and the region. And having assembled the army he made his way towards him (Theodore).

6. Throughout the night, the saint, devoting himself to prayer, tearfully made mental supplication to God to grant him his purpose. Then, having briefly fallen into a heavy sleep, he saw the roof of the chamber where he was resting divided in the middle and a light came down from above and shone all about the room; and he heard a voice say, 'Take courage, Theodore, for I am with you, your God who knew you before time and bears witness to you.'[189] Trembling at this light and full of joy he stood up, and then once more having devoted himself to prayer, he became as steel in his piety. But already, as the impious Licinius approached the city, that just man, having stretched up his hands and eyes to God, again made a more extensive supplication, saying, 'God and emperor of all, the sweet refuge of those who depend on you, look on my shattered heart with merciful and gracious eyes and do not leave me, who is not yet ready to fight to the last, to the anger of a mortal emperor, an emperor who does not want to know [171] you, the God who is emperor over all and in all; but in accordance with your truthful promise, be with us, those who know and confess you as creator and guardian of all creation. Let your flowing water spring forth in me and when I open my mouth let your word be given to me and my mind be well-founded in you, the cornerstone. Keep me in confession of you, O Lord, until my very last breath, and may an angel shining with your glory

---

189 'Take courage, Theodore'. Cf. above, p. 86, n. 104; Niketas Paphlag., *Encomium* 85. 4–6. In the martyrdom of Theodore the Recruit the saint hears God's voice after his trial had commenced and while he is imprisoned.

take my soul, wholly washed and cleansed of every spot of sin with the
blood of your witness.'

7. In this way he prayed and commended himself to God, and then, robing
himself in a spotless garment, he mounted a horse and left to meet the
emperor. When they came within sight of one another, they straight away
came together with salutations and embraced each other.[190] Everyone was
amazed, even Licinius himself, I say, at the appearance of Theodore – divine
in countenance and decorous in manner, free in spirit and a most noble
presence. And as he entered the city, the noise and clamour of dancing and
acclamations arose, caused by the pleasure of the imperial entrance. The
emperor, having ordered all to be silent, began a speech to them in these
words: 'Blessings, and all other good things to you, men of the city; for a
city renowned and famous, a people compliant to the gods and obedient to
the laws, this is also the paternal inheritance of your upbringing; but you
are even more praiseworthy for having elected this man' – indicating to
them the holy Theodore – 'to have by you; and while his fame has reached
us and heralded him as good, yet the man is superior to his reputation.'
And with embraces and salutations he glorified the saint, and then took
his hand, saying, 'Come hither, dear friend; let us first together show piety
to the gods, and then the discussion of the relevant matters will no doubt
follow.' And the saint replied, 'You spoke fittingly, [172] O emperor, but if
you would hear us, perhaps my words will also be acceptable to you.' And
the emperor said, 'What? Did you not yet know my disposition concerning
you?' And Theodore said, 'I did know, yet I have not yet made trial of
myself, but if you would permit me to go alone to the gods, then indeed I
shall come to the test.' Licinius said, 'What is prohibiting you from coming
with us?' And the martyr said, 'First, o emperor, I wish to take them home
and treat them in the most appropriate manner and appease them with
prayers and private sacrifices; and then with you and the multitude I will
go before them.' Bringing out the gods made of silver and gold that he had,
the emperor gave them to the martyr, adding, 'But pray for us as well.' And

---

190 The account of the meeting between the emperor and Theodore appears to follow
the established pattern for local commanders to receive an imperial visit in the ninth or
tenth century. See the description of the imperial cortège arriving in the provinces in Const.
Porph., *Three treatises*, (B) 92–100, 122–128; (C) 443–473, with commentary; there are also
parallels here, particularly in the opening exchange of greetings, with the account of the visit
of the emperor to the borderer Digenis: see Chapter 1, n. 36 above; *Digenis*: IV. 971–1053;
Trapp 1971: G.IV. 1922–2004.

so, having taken away the false and laughable gods, and having smashed them to pieces, the great saint brought them as another sort of sacrifice to the true God, distributing them to those in need.[191]

8. Two days passed and the emperor summoned the saint. And when he came, the emperor said, 'Let the gods come, Theodore, to receive the sacrifices performed by you with us and the multitude.' And the saint said, 'If they are indeed gods, let them come by themselves or not.' Licinius said, 'We should serve the gods.' And the saint answered, 'But those gods neither come when called upon, nor do they hearken when served by others.'[192] And the emperor said, 'We should not think about these things, Theodore; their understanding is greater than ours; we should only honour the gods and venerate them with sacrifices, according to our law and tradition.' In response to these words, the saint fell silent with a smile. And the emperor said, 'What is your intention? Why do you stall for time, Theodore?' And turning to those who were present, he said, 'What happened? Why is he silent?'

9. As they were all considering this development in surprise, and were staring fixedly at the saint, a certain Maxentius,[193] [173] holding the rank of centurion, having discovered the martyr's conduct towards the gods, said, 'For my part I would not want to keep quiet about what I have seen, O emperor. For what has been done by this man's actions regarding the gods is painful to know, and unbearable to hear with one's ears.' And the emperor said, 'What is this? Speak truthfully.' Then the centurion said, 'I think this man is not favourably disposed towards you or the gods, O emperor, indeed he disrespects both the gods and you. Why should I not speak clearly about what has happened? I myself saw the head of the great goddess Artemis in the market broken into many pieces. This man is the one who broke it up with his audacious right hand.'[194] Hearing these things, the emperor, filled

191 Cf. Ps. 74. 13–14. Whereas Theodore the Recruit burns down the temple (of Artemis), the General takes the idols away and cuts them up before distributing the pieces to the poor.
192 Cf. Ps. 115. 4–8.
193 Maxentios fulfils the role here of the informant in the passions of Theodore the Recruit; the author probably deliberately used a 'Roman' name to maintain the 'ancient' ambience of the text.
194 The head of a pagan god was a particular target of (Christian) divine anger, cf. the bolt of lightning that struck the head of the image of Apollo when the emperor Julian moved the remains of St Babylas: Chrysostom, *Homily on Babylas*: Schatkin et al. 2004: §3.

with rage and dismay, looked at the martyr with great pain and grief, saying, 'What about this, Theodore? What of what has been said? Where are the gods that we entrusted to you? Did you sacrifice to them as you promised to do and did you bring what is necessary for their worship?'

10. Then the saint, casting aside the pretence, judging that it was no longer time for silence, nor for any concealment, nor for hiding his light under a bushel but rather for placing it on the lampstand,[195] and for making his confession clear to the lord, said: 'No, by the truth. Not only did I not sacrifice, but I gladly rejected the empty and the foolish, and prepared to make them useful in another way, distributing them to the poor. Your decision was the authority to act. For of old I knew and understood the feebleness of these things and I pitied the senselessness of those who worshipped those gods. Moreover, emperor, I also know to what extent you are the cause of foolishness in these matters. Have a little patience, therefore, with those of yours who care for the truth and, hearkening to those offering sensible counsel, deceive yourself no longer, but rather recognise the true God, through whom you have life and imperial power by divine dispensation, who himself rejects veneration of ignoble gods as impious, gods that are not able to protect themselves, let alone those who worship them, [174] just as they cannot punish those who set them at nought and mock them, who are numerous. And the proof is right here, if you please: for I insulted and mocked them – and treated them as was fitting. So let them punish the offender if they can.' The martyr wanted to prolong his speech further, but the emperor, growing angry because of his friend's unexpected change of mind, said, 'Alas for our foolishness, our wrong-mindedness – giving heed to such a man, I meet with such a deceit as his. And this depraved man, mocking not only ourselves but also the gods, escaped notice. But for my part I will exact just punishment from you, who disdained this charity, inflicting such penalties on you, that they will be sufficient to repay your insult to the gods and perhaps to us.' And, straightaway, turning towards the public executioners, he said, 'Bring out the whips; let the guilty one be stripped; scourge him cruelly; let him be deemed worthy of neither pity nor mercy; and then let his neck be pounded with leaden balls.'[196]

---

195 Cf. Matt. 5. 15.
196 This appears to have involved a form of whipping or beating with a lead-weighted lash or staff. The author probably borrowed the motif from the *Acta Nerei et Achillei*, 16. 18 (§17); cf. Lampe 1961: 1352, s.v. σφαῖρα (*sphaira*).

11. In saying such things, the impious man revealed the extraordinary nature of his anger through his eyes and teeth, and with shouts and threats urged on the torturers. And after the saint was stripped, his hands along with his feet were stretched forcibly apart, and when he had been flogged, his limbs were torn asunder, his hands were dislocated, his veins gushed blood, the joints of his spine were loosened by the heavy blows of the weighted balls. And so, as the saint was suffering in this way, he already laboured to draw short and feeble breaths and was about to give up his soul; just then Licinius' rage abated and he ordered the torturers to release the saint. And when he had been spared their blows for a little while, he revived a little, was able to draw breath, and began to believe that he would live. At that point rage seized the emperor once more and he said, 'Actually, let him live; in a word, let him come round, the cursed, foul, abominable one, who has raged against the gods themselves; let him be lacerated by iron hooks and let his remaining limbs [175] be scorched by the fiercest of fires.' And as he said these words the hooks and the fire were applied. And some of the torturers lacerated him, others brought on the flame. But the martyr was spiritually refreshed by the dew of the divine spirit. Therefore the tyrant, as if bantering with the saint, said, 'Bring out sharp stones for the better treatment of him who plays the man; for we see that he is very pleasantly disposed towards the torments that are inflicted upon him.' And at the same time, looking at the martyr with a sneer, he said, 'I know, Theodore, that the prescribed torture affected you greatly, even though you pretended not to feel it, wishing to attribute this to the power of your God and to deceive the foolish; but the sharpness of the stones that has now been imposed upon you will affect you very much and reveal all your pretences.'

12. Licinius spoke thus because his heart was wicked and altogether far from God. The martyr of Christ, however, benefiting from the powerful influence from on high, neither uttered a sound while he was being rent asunder, nor was he seen to groan nor to show any sorrowful countenance or any sign of weakness at all. And indeed Licinius, feigning a certain compassion, ordered the saint to be released; and turning to him he said, 'Do you still abide by your previous words, Theodore, or has a change of mind and better thoughts come over you?' And the martyr said, 'Do you really think to change my mind or to alter the foundation of my trust in Christ? – what an absurdity! For what harm have the blows done to me, except to make me stronger?' And one of the bystanders said, 'But put aside such great folly and your reckless argument with the emperor – ';

'Release me from living first,' said the martyr, 'if indeed you wish me to remain silent, since as long as my soul is within me, no fear will keep me from speaking the truth.' And the emperor said, 'To expect something sensible and pious from such an unholy soul is clear folly; therefore I order this man to be held for the present under a secure guard.' [176] And he spoke and it was granted. Except he did not allow him to rest, but commanded certain people to go into the prison to trick him with clever words and fraud and to employ every trick and zeal into shaking his resistance. And so, since the prison held the saint fast, the imitator of Christ submitted thus quietly, making supplication on behalf of his tormentors, praying for droplets of the knowledge of God to seep into them, and with regard to those who tried to change his mind, adducing that great nonsense, he acted like David: for *he was as a man that hears not, and who has no reproofs in his mouth.*[197]

13. Five days passed, and having learned that the saint had not changed his mind, the emperor commanded that a wooden cross be set up in the middle of the place called *Basilikē*,[198] and that the saint be placed on it and nailed to it. He then said: 'Any devotees of the gods who can draw bows should loose arrows at him. And apart from these, anyone who can invent another terrible punishment that can reach his soul, he will be a friend to me and gratify me greatly. May my eyes no longer behold this villain still alive, for the mere sight of him is a burden and a scourge touching my heart.' And when he said these things, the saint was brought out of the prison, pierced and foully abused, yet not submitting to anything that could cause pain from the great tortures, until the tormentors reached the place and set up the cross, and stretched out and nailed up the champion. Then a hail of arrows was shot by many people at his naked flesh, immediately piercing and covering his body all over with wounds. Behold the excess of savagery and frenzy! For, yanking the arrows out of his flesh, two and three times they loosed them at the saint; nor did this suffice for the sons of darkness, the workers of lawlessness,[199] but there was always something newer to be devised following the wicked injunction of Licinius. [177] So, therefore, he who from the beginning has been the slayer of mankind and enemy of the common race of men [i.e.

197 Cf. Ps. 37. 14.
198 'Royal' or 'imperial'.
199 Cf. Matt. 7. 23.

the Devil] established a violent chastisement, a punishment not bearable to be heard by the ear alone; for what they thought up, the true friends of the demons, who were initiated by them, carried out. Removing the saint's loincloth, they touched his private parts and — O blood-stained hands, O soul most savage and shameless — taking a very sharp iron nail, they drove it into the passage of the member.[200] And then drawing it out and inserting the nail repeatedly, they were neither horrified, nor did they feel pain, nor were they disgusted. The martyr, feeling the sharper sensation in this unendurable excess of pain, cried loudly, 'Christ, help me. See what I suffer and how sharp pangs oppress and cause pain to my soul.[201] The perils of Hades found me, *iron passed through my soul.*[202] Let my relief and my release be in the manifestation of your shining forth; my fervent joy, rescue me from those surrounding me. When will I come and be seen by your face?'[203]

14. While the martyr prayed thus, and those mocking and imposing terrible pains, thinking that the saint had already breathed his last, were coming back, a divine power came to him from heaven and a voice full of joy was heard saying, 'Rejoice, brave champion of Christ: you glorified through your limbs[204] He who endured the cross for your sake. You completed your journey, you kept your faith. Henceforward, the crown of justice is reserved for you, eternal life and joy await you.' Thus it spoke and immediately departed, and with the voice every welt and every scar and pain and any feelings of distress also departed, and he was fully restored to health, of good cheer, full of joy, and full of grace. Then his lips moved to sing the hymn of fervent joy: 'I will exalt You, my king and my God, and I will praise Your name for eternity, that for me *weeping shall tarry for the evening, but* [178] *joy shall be in the morning.* The Lord is great and highly to be praised and there is nothing beyond His majesty.'[205] And thus through the whole night he conversed with God with all his mind and voice and rejoiced in His beauty.

---

200 I.e. into the urethra.
201 See Ps. 42.10; Ps. 10. 1. On the sado-eroticism of such tortures and their socio-cultural functions see, in particular, Frankfurter 2009 with literature and detailed discussion.
202 A variation on Ps. 105. 18: σίδηρον διῆλθεν ἡ ψυχὴ αὐτοῦ ('his soul passed into iron').
203 See Ps. 109. 26–27; Ps. 25. 6–7; Ps. 31. 7–8, 15–16.
204 ἐν τοῖς μέλεσι: a play on the words: 'through your limbs' (because of the torture) and 'through your music/songs' (a metaphor for his suffering).
205 Ps. 30. 5; 12.

15. But Licinius, having already arisen as the day was dawning, sent out two of those who held the post of centurion, Antiochus and Patricius by name, having ordered them to drag the body of the martyr dishonorably before him – for how did he imagine he still lived, covered with blows, drenched in violence? – so that he might thoroughly exult over it and mock it even after death; and then he commanded that it be cast into the sea, so that it might not receive fitting burial. Accordingly, when they were near the place where they had affixed the saint to the stake, looking intently, they saw the stake, and yet, looking around in every direction, they did not see the saint. Thereupon a reminiscence of Christ's resurrection from the dead troubled them. And so Antiochus, speaking up, said, 'Is it possible, friend Patricius, that the sayings of the Christians that the crucified Christ was raised from the dead are true, and so indeed His servant Theodore has come to life again and arisen? For know that I saw him yesterday pierced with arrows and nailed to this very stake, nearly dead and hardly different from a corpse. Now then, unless the corpse has been stolen, what else is to be thought?' And while they were saying such things to each other, the blessed Theodore appeared to them, a psalm still on his lips, and showing in the joy of his eyes and the brightness of his face the grace in his soul, and he said to them: 'Children, I am Theodore; do not be afraid. God the avenging Lord, the avenging God, who cares for your salvation and who calls you to Himself, has resurrected me against all expectation when I was already at the gates of death. If, therefore, you have faith, you shall see greater things than these.'[206] [179] Having spoken thus, he placed the sign of the divine cross upon them, though they were still in doubt and unbelief. And thereupon, filled with divine grace and just as if their eyes had been opened, they cried out, 'Great is the God of the Christians.' And straight away in prostration they clasped his feet and begged him to give them access to Christ. 'For we will no longer turn away,' they said, 'nor will we be slaves to error, nor will we deliver ourselves unto the darkness, having come to believe that we should worship the one God who is proclaimed by you.' The holy Theodore, therefore, recognising that they believed with their whole hearts, not only approached them but embraced them and said to them with great joy, 'But do not disbelieve, since what happened to me, happened for the sake of your salvation, so that you should know and recognise and speak truly: your conversion comes from the right hand of the Most High[207] – who is

206 Cf. John 1. 50.
207 Ps. 44. 3; Ps. 77.10.

even now present among you, unseen, recording your confessions. Let him therefore be the light of your souls, burning always, so that the Devil, the enemy of all, may not pervert your hearts and make them go back again to walk in idolatry.' Saying such things and more, he strengthened their souls and set their hearts in the foundation of faith. And as the story of the miracle spread in every direction, showing to all that he was living and healthy and unharmed, others also approached, eighty-five in number, chosen men and distinguished by their wisdom; and when they saw him, they also believed and fell down before the saint, praying that they too might be counted among the company of believers; and when they had been instructed in the word of salvation, they were released from all transient things, and within a short time they exhibited great progress in matters of the faith. For no longer did they simply believe, but became also of the party of those who are persecuted in the name of Christ.

16. When Licinius learned what had occurred, he sent a certain Cestus, one of the patricians, having supplied him with a larger body of soldiers, [180] ordering him to put to death by the sword all those who had come to believe in Christ through the martyr. But while Licinius – who was extremely malicious and not readily cured where evil was concerned – was ordering these things, Cestus went off and after having both observed the situation and had his soul filled with reconsiderations, as if a divine ray of light had illuminated him, he became himself a member of the confraternity of believers, and with him all the soldiers, each closely following the other, like a chain, shouting together: 'One God, Christ, saving those who believe in Him: let both the emperor and the people who share his madness hear this.' For this reason there then took place a riot and an unstoppable uprising of the rest of the people of the city. And a certain swordsman of the imperial bodyguards, rushing as though to strike the martyr, was struck by Cestus, who could not bear with indifference the shameless act against the martyr; but another man, named Merpas, having mortally struck Cestus himself, sent that martyr to Christ with a single blow. And many more people would have been slaughtered if the soldier of Christ, Theodore, who was practiced in [Christ's] gentleness, had not arrived, and both by his service to those already injured, as well as by the gentleness and kindness of his spirit, checked the violence of the populace on the one hand, lest they venture headstrong deeds, while on the other hand he instructed the believers in Christ to endure all that was happening with magnanimity, exchanging not evil with evil but rather with good. And persuaded by him they eagerly

gave themselves to slaughter, content to become willing sacrifices for the first victim offered as a sacrifice to the Father on our account.

17. When Licinius had heard that many of his soldiers were submitting to Christ and Theodore, and that the fortunes of the martyr were increasing, whereas his fortunes were utterly decreasing, he ordered some other soldiers, those indeed whom he trusted most, to come and not simply to leave it to chance, but [181] to seize Theodore, and without making any excuses whatsoever, to slay him. But when they arrived at the place, the crowd of believers did not allow them to kill the saint, each one offering his own neck in his stead. The saint, rebuking them, held back their rush, saying 'Children, let not those whom I begot in Christ, as Paul says,[208] in any way hinder me this day, which I have desired already for a long time; nor, thinking to do something good, begrudge me the greatest act, martyrdom for Christ, which is entirely impossible unless it be in a death attained for Him. But it is good for you to have the peace of Christ which, as he ascended to the Father, he bequeathed to his own first disciples, and through them, to all.'[209] And so he commanded those who had already turned away from error and who recognised the Creator of all, to guard their faith in Him unchanging to the end, saying 'For he who stands firm to the end will be saved; even if you live under emperors and rulers, fear nothing; for *He is faithful who promised*[210] *I will never leave you nor forsake you.*'[211] But to those who were not yet delivered from idolatrous error, he said, 'But if still the veil of impiety has not yet been taken away from your hearts, I have confidence in Christ that divine grace will shine upon many of you and draw you towards it; merely live peacefully with one another and adhere carefully to love of neighbour and supply those who are in need according to your means; the command of Christ and the very law of nature teaches this.' And, speaking thus, uniting the whole multitude in one fitting reflection in common, blessing and offering prayers for all as was appropriate, he charged his servant, who was taking note of everything, to distribute all his possessions to the poor, the widows, and the orphans,[212] after his departure to God, and to bury his body in

208 1 Corinthians 4:15.
209 Cf. John 14. 27.
210 Hebrews 10:23.
211 Hebrews 13:5.
212 One might compare the martyr's actions here with those of tenth- and eleventh-century Byzantine aristocrats who did likewise.

the territory of Euchaïna, in a place that [182] came down to him through paternal inheritance. Having given these instructions, he bowed his head with dignity and, as many stood by, looking down upon his grace and his eagerness for death, and gaining thereby firm assurances about that which is to come, his blessed head was severed with a sword.

18. Lifting up his holy remains, they laid them to rest as an inviolate treasure in Euchaïna as indeed had been prescribed to them, an extraordinary richness, a treasure salvific for the inhabitants of the town, a place of refuge against all diseases, to the glory of the great God and of our saviour Jesus Christ, to whom belongs all honour, glory and magnificence now and forever. Amen.

BIBLIOGRAPHY

Sources, collections of sources and reference works

Acta Nerei et Achillei ed. Achelis, H. *Acta SS. Nerei et Achillei* (*TU* 11, 2. Leipzig, 1893): 1–23 (*BHG* 1327)

Acta Polycarpi Holmes, M.W. *The Apostolic Fathers: Greek texts and English translations* (Grand Rapids, MI, 2007): 298–333 (text 306–333); also ed. A.P. Orbán and S. Ronchey, in A.A.R. Bastiaensen et al., eds, *Atti e passioni dei martiri* (Milan, 1987): 371–381 (*BHG* 1556–1560)

Anastasi, R. 1984. *Giovanni Mauropode, metropolita di Euchaïta, Canzoniere* (Catania)

Anastasius Sin. *Anastasii Sinaitae Quaestiones et responsiones*, ed. M. Richard and J. Munitiz (Corpus Christianorum. Series Graeca, 59) (Brepols, 2006)

Aufhauser, J.B. 1913. ed. *Miracula S. Georgii* (Leipzig) (*BHG* 687–691x)

Briscoe, J. 1998. ed. *Valerii Maximi Facta et dicta memorabilia*, 2 vols (Stuttgart)

Cedrenus, *Compendium historiarum*, ed. I. Bekker, 2 vols (CSHB) (Bonn, 1838–1839)

Const. Porph. *Three treatises* *Constantine Porphyrogenitus, Three Treatises on Imperial Military Expeditions*, ed., English trans. and commentary J.F. Haldon (CFHB 28) (Vienna, 1990)

Conybeare, F.C. 1896. *The Armenian Apology and Acts of Apollonius and Other Monuments of Early Christianity* (London): 220–237 (Armenian passion of St Theodore *stratēlatēs*, trans. from *Vitae et Passiones Sanctorum Selectae ex Eclogariis*, 2 vols [Venice, 1874], I: 569–581)

Darrouzès, J. 1960. *Épistoliers byzantins du Xe siècle* (Archives de l'Orient chrétien 6) (Paris)

Darrouzès, J. 1981. *Notitiae Episcopatuum Ecclesiae Constantinopolitanae* (Paris)

Dawes, E.A.S. and N. Baynes. 1948. *Three Byzantine saints; contemporary biographies, trans. from the Greek* (Oxford)

De Lagarde, P. 1882. *Iohannis Euchaitorum metropolitae quae in codice vaticano graeco 676 supersunt* (Göttingen), revised ed. I. Bollig (Amsterdam, 1976)

Delehaye, H. 1909. *Les légendes grecques des saints militaires* (Paris)

Delehaye, H. 1925a. 'De Sancto Theodoro martyre Euchaïtis Helenoponti', in *AS Nov.* IV (Brussels): 11–89

De Them.   *Costantino Porfirogenito, De Thematibus*, ed. A. Pertusi (Studi e Testi 160) (Città del Vaticano, 1952)

Deubner, L. 1900. *De Incubatione capita quattuor* (Leipzig): 120–134

Digenis   Jeffreys, E.M. 1998. ed. and trans. *Digenis Akritis: the Grottaferrata and Escorial versions* (Cambridge)

Eustratius   *Eustratii presbyteri Constantinipolitani, De statu animarum post mortem*, ed. P. Van Deun (CCSG 60) (Turnhout, 2006)

Fernandez Marcos, N. 1975. *Los thaumata di Sofronio, contribucion al estudio de la "incubatio" Cristiana* (Madrid)

Flusin, B. 1992. *Saint Anastase le Perse et l'histoire de la Palestine au début du VIIe siècle*, I: *Les textes*; II, *Commentaire* (Paris) (see *BHG* 84–90)

Franchi Dei Cavalieri, P. 1912. 'Passio S. Theagenis', *Note agiografiche* 1 (Rome): 179–185 (*BHG* 749)

Greek Anthology   W.R. Paton, *The Greek Anthology, with an English translation by W.R. Paton*, 5 vols (Cambridge, MA, 1960)

Gregory of Nyssa, *Sermons*   ed. J.P. Cavarnos, *Gregory of Nyssa, Sermons* II, 1 (Leiden–New York 1990): 61–71; trans. J. Leemans, 'Gregory of Nyssa: a homily on Theodore the recruit', in J. Leemans, W. Mayer, P. Allen and B. Demandschutter, eds, *'Let us die that we may live': Greek homilies on Christian martyrs from Asia Minor, Palestine and Syria c. 350–450 A.D.* (London 2003): 82–90 (*BHG* 1760)

Grumel–Darrouzès 1989 Grumel, V. 1972. *Les Regestes des actes du Patriarcat de Constantinople*, i: *les actes des Patriarches* i: *Les regestes de 381 à 715* (Chalcedon, 1932/2nd rev. edn J. Darrouzès, Paris, 1972); ii and iii: *Les Regestes de 715 à 1206* (Chalcedo,n 1936, 1947 [Bucharest]); 2nd rev. edn J. Darrouzès (Paris, 1989)

Halkin, F. 1962. 'Un opuscule inconnu du magistre Nicéphore Ouranos (Vie de Saint Théodore le Conscrit)', *AB* 80: 308–324, text: 313–323 (repr. in F. Halkin, *Martyrs grecs IIe–VIIIes.* [London, 1974])

Halkin F. 1981. 'L'éloge de saint Théodore le Stratélate par Euthyme Protasecretis', *AB* 99: 221–237

Honigmann, E. 1939. ed. *Le Synekdémos d'Hiéroklès et l'opuscule géographique de Georges de Chypre* (Corpus Bruxellense Historiae Byzantinae I) (Brussels)

Itinera Hierosolymitana saeculi IIII–VIII, ed. P. Geyer (*Corpus Scriptorum Ecclesiasticorum Latinorum* 39) (Vienna, 1898)

John Moschus, *Pratum spirituale*, in *PG* 87/3, 2352–3112; trans. J. Wortley, *The spiritual meadow, by John Moschos (also known as John Eviratus)*. Introduction, translation (Kalamazoo, MI, 1992)

Just., *Edict.*   in Just., *Nov.*

Just., *Nov.*   Justinian, *Novellae constitutions*, in *Corpus Juris Civilis*, I: *Institutiones*, ed. P. Krüger; *Digesta*, ed. Th. Mommsen; II: *Codex Iustinianus*, ed. P. Krüger; III: *Novellae*, eds R. Schöll, W. Kroll (Berlin, 1892–1895, repr. 1945–1963)

Lampe, G.W.H. 1961. *A patristic Greek lexicon* (Oxford)

Laurent, V. 1963, 1965, 1972. *Le corpus des sceaux de l'empire byzantin*, V, 1–3: *l'Église* (Paris)

Leo diac.   *Leonis diaconi Caloensis Historiae libri decem*, ed. C.B. Hase (CSHB) (Bonn, 1828); English trans. and commentary: A.-M. Talbot, D. Sullivan, *The History of Leo the Deacon* (Washington DC, 2005)

Lübeck, K. 1910. 'Der hl. Theodor als Erbe des Gottes Men', *Der Katholik* 90: 199–215

Malalas   *Ioannis Malalae Chronographia*, ed. H. Thurn (CFHB 35) (Berlin and New York, 2000); English trans. E. Jeffreys, M. Jeffreys and R. Scott, *The Chronicle of John Malalas* (Byzantina Australiensia 4) (Melbourne, 1986)

Matthew of Edessa   *Chronique de Matthieu d'Edesse*, trans. E. Dulaurier (Paris, 1858)

Mauropous, *Letters*   Karpozilos, A. 1990. *The Letters of Ioannes Mauropous Metropolitan of Euchaïta* (CFHB 34) (Thessalonica)

Miracula S. Demetrii   ed. P. Lemerle, *Les plus anciens recueils des miracles de saint Démétrius et la pénétration des Slaves dans les Balkans*, 1: *Le texte* (Paris 1979)

Miracles of St Thekla   ed. G. Dagron, *Vie et Miracles de Sainte Thècle: texte grec, traduction et commentaire* (Brussels 1978); trans. S. Johnson, in Talbot, A.-M. and S. Johnson, *Miracle tales from Byzantium* (Dumbarton Oaks Medieval Library) (Cambridge, MA–London): vii–xiv, 1–201 (cf. *BHG* 1710–1722)

Nedungatt, G. and M. Featherstone. 1995. *The Council in Trullo revisited* (Rome)

Nesbitt, J. and V. Crisafulli. 1997. *The Miracles of Saint Artemius: Translation, Commentary and Analysis* (Washington DC) (*BHG* 173)

Niketas Paphlag., *Encomium*   *Laudatio S. Theodori Ducis a Niceta Paphlagone*, ed. H. Delehaye, in *AS Nov.* IV: 80–89

Nov. Val.   *Novellae constitutiones Valentiniani Augusti*, in *CTh.*

Passio S. Nicetae in H. Delehaye, 'Saints de Thrace et de Mésie', *AB* 31 (1912): 161–300 (text: 209–215, comm: 281–287) (*BHG* 1339)

Passio SS. Eutropii, Cleonici et Basilisci in Delehaye 1909: 202–213 (*BHG* 656)

Patria CP   Th. Preger. ed. *Patria Constantinopoleos* (*Scriptores Originum Constantinopolitanarum* 2) (Leipzig, 1907/New York, 1975)

Pitra, J.B. 1876. 'Theodori Studitae, De s. Theodoro duce', in J.B. Pitra, *Analecta sacra* I (Paris): 361–365 (*BHG* 1753a)

Proc., *Buildings* in Procopius, *Works*, vol. 7, ed. and trans. H.B. Dewing. (Loeb Classical Library) (New York, 1914–1940)

Rhalles, K. and M. Potles. 1852–1859. Σύνταγμα τῶν θείων καὶ ἱερῶν κανόνων, 6 vols (Athens)

Rupprecht, E. 1935. *Cosmae et Damiani sanctorum medicorum vita et miracula* (Berlin) (*BHG* 373b)

Seeck, O. 1876. *Notitia dignitatum utriusque imperii* (Leipzig)

Sigalas, A. 1921. *Des Chrysippos von Jerusalem Enkomion auf den hl. Theodoros Teron* (Leipzig–Berlin) (*BHG* 1765c)

Sigalas, A. 1924. Ἡ διασκευὴ τῶν ὑπὸ Χρυσίππου παραδεδομένων θαυμάτων τοῦ ἁγίου Θεοδώρου', *EEBS* 1: 295–339

Sigalas, A. 1925. Ἀνωνύμου Βίος καὶ ἀνατροφὴ τοῦ ἁγίου Θεοδώρου τοῦ Τήρωνος', *EEBS* 2: 220–226 (*BHG* 1765)

Sigalas, A. 1937. *Des Chrysippos von Jerualem Enkomion auf den hl. Johannes den Täufer. Textkritische erstmalige Ausgabe mit einem Anhang: Untersuchungen und Ergänzungen zu den Schriften des Chrysippos* (Athens)

Strabo   *The geography of Strabo*, 8 vols (Cambridge, MA, 1923)

Synax. CP   *Synaxarium Constantinopolitanum*, ed. H. Delehaye (Propylaeum ad AS Novembris) (Brussels, 1902)

Talbot, A.-M. and D. Sullivan. 2005. *The History of Leo the deacon* (Washington DC)

Theod. Lect. *HE*   *Historia ecclesiastica*, ed. G.C. Hansen, *Kirchengeschichte* (Berlin, 1971)

Theoph.   *Theophanis Chronographia*, ed. C. de Boor, 2 vols (Leipzig 1883, 1885); *The Chronicle of Theophanes Confessor*, trans. C. Mango and R. Scott (Oxford, 1997)

Trapp, E. 1971. *Digenes Akrites. Synoptische Ausgabe der ältesten Versionen* (Wiener Byzantinistische Studien VII) (Vienna)

TT (Tapu Tahrir Defter) 387   *387 Numaralı Muhâsebe-i Vilâyet-i Karaman ve Rûm Defteri* (937/1530) (Osmanlı Arşivi Daire Başkanlığı Yayın Nu: 36. Defter-i Hâkânı Dizisi: III) (Ankara, 1997)

Usener, H. 1886. 'Acta S. Marinae et S. Christophori', in *Festschrift zur fünften Säcularfeier der Karl-Rupprechts-Universität zu Heidelberg* (Bonn): 56–76

Van Hooff, G. 1883. 'Acta graeca S. Theodori ducis martyris, nunc primum edita', *AB* 2: 359–367 (*BHG* 1750)

Vita Alypii Stylita   ed. H. Delehaye, *Les saints stylites* (Subsid. Hag. 14) (Brussels, 1923): 148–169 (*BHG* 65)

Vita Euthymii   ed. E. Schwartz, *Kyrillos von Skythopolis* (*TU* 49/2) (Leipzig, 1939): 3–85 (*BHG* 647–648b)

Vita Euthymii Iunioris, ed. L. Petit, 'Vie et office de S. Euthyme le jeune', *ROC* 8 (1903): 155–205 (repr. L. Clugnet, in *Bibliotheca Hagiographica Orientalis* 5 [1904]: 14–51) (*BHG* 655)

Vita Eutychii.   *Vita Eutychii Archiepiscopi Constantinopolitani*, in: *PG* 86/2, 2273–2390 (*BHG* 657)

Vita Lazari Gales.   *Vita S. Lazari monachi in monte Galesio*, in *AS Nov.* III (Brussels): 508–588; English trans. of vita with commentary: R.P.H. Greenfield, *An eleventh century pillar saint: the Life of Lazaros of Mt. Galesion* (Washington DC, 2000) (*BHG* 979)

Vita Porphyrii Gazensis ed. H. Grégoire and M.A. Kugener, *Marc le Diacre, Vie de*

Porphyre (Paris, 1930); English trans. G.F. Hill, *The Life of Porphyry, bishop of Gaza* (Oxford, 1913) (*BHG* 1570)

Vita S. Sabae ed. E. Schwartz, *Kyrillos von Skythopolis* (Texte und Untersuchungen 49, 2) (Leipzig, 1939): 85–200 (*BHG* 1608)

Vita Theod. Syk. *Vie de Théodore de Sykéon*, ed. and trans. A. Festugière, 2 vols (Subsid. Hag. 48) (Brussels, 1970); English trans. with commentary: E. Dawes and N.H. Baynes, *Three Byzantine saints. Contemporary biographies of St Daniel the Stylite, St Theodore of Sykeon and St John the Almsgiver* (Oxford, 1948): 87–192 (*BHG* 1748)

Winstedt, E.O. 1910. *Coptic Texts on St Theodore the General, on St Theodore the Eastern, on Chamoul and Justus* (London): 73–133

Zonaras *Ioannis Zonarae epitomae historiarum libri XIII usque ad XVIII*, ed. Th. Büttner-Wobst (CSHB) (Bonn, 1897)

Literature

Abrahamse, D. 1967. *Hagiographic sources for Byzantine cities 500–900 A.D.* (Ann Arbor, MI)

Altenburger, M. and F. Mann, 1988. *Bibliographie zu Gregor von Nyssa. Editionen – Übersetzungen – Literatur* (Leiden–New York)

Amélineau, E. 1888. 'Fragments coptes pour server à l'histoire de la conquête del'Egypte par les Arabes', *Journal Asiatique*, 8e série, 12: 361–410

Anastasi, R. 1976. 'Su Giovanni d'Euchaïta', *Siculorum Gymnasium* 29: 19–49

Anderson, J.G.C. 1897. 'The road system of eastern Asia Minor with the evidence of Byzantine campaigns', *Journal of Hellenic Studies* 17: 22–30

Anderson, J.G.C. 1900. 'Pontica III. The correspondence between Abgar of Edessa and Christ', *Journal of Hellenic Studies* 20: 156–158

Anderson, J.G.C. 1903. *Studia Pontica* I. *A Journey of Exploration in Pontus* (Brussels)

Anderson, J.G.C., F. Cumont and H. Grégoire. 1910. *Studia Pontica* III. *Recueil des inscriptions grecques et latines du Pont et de l'Arménie* (Brussels)

André, A. 1891. 'Der hl. Theodor von Amasia nach der armenischen Legende', *Die Katholischen Missionen*: 225–30

Anrich, G. 1917. *Hagios Nikolaos: der heilige Nikolaos in der griechischen Kirche*, 2 (Leipzig–Berlin)

Antonopoulou, Th. 2009. 'The metrical Passions of SS. Theodore Tiron and Theodore Stratelates in cod. Laura Λ 170 and the *grammatikos* Merkourios', in S. Kotzabassi and G. Mavromatis, eds, *Realia Byzantina* (*Byzantinisches Archiv* 22) (Berlin–New York): 1–11

Ariantzi, D. 2012. *Kindheit in Byzanz: emotionale, geistige und materielle Entwicklung im familiären Umfeld vom 6. bis zum 11. Jahrhundert* (Boston–Berlin)

Arnold, C.E. 1995. *The Colossian syncretism. The interface between Christianity and folk belief at Colossae* (Wissenschaftliche Untersuchungen zum Neuen Testament 2.77) (Tübingen)

Artun, T. 2008. 'The Miracles of St Theodore Tērōn: an eighth-century source?', *JöB* 58: 1–11

Aufhauser, J.B. 1911. *Das Drachenwunder des heiligen Georg* (Byzantinisches Archiv 5) (Leipzig)

Auzépy, M.-F. 2008. 'State of emergency (700–850)', in J. Shepard, ed., *Cambridge History of the Byzantine empire ca. 500–1492* (Cambridge): 251–291

Barnes, T.D. 1968. 'Legislation against the Christians', *JRS* 58: 32–50

Barnish, S. 1985. 'The Wealth of Iulianus Argentarius', *B* 55: 5–38

Beard, M. 1994. 'The Roman and the foreign: the cult of the 'Great Mother' in imperial Rome', in N. Thomas and C. Humphrey, eds, *Shamanism, History, and the State* (Ann Arbor, MI): 164–90

Beaucamp, J. 1983. 'L'allaitement: mère ou nourrice?', *JöB* 32.2: 549–558 (= Akten des XVI. Internationalen Byzantinistenkongresses II/2)

Beck, H.-G. 1959. *Kirche und theologische Literatur im byzantinischen Reich* (Handbuch der Altertumswissenschaft xii, 2.1 = Byzantinisches Handbuch 2.1) (Munich)

Belke, K. 1984. (with M. Restle), *Tabula Imperii Byzantini 4: Galatien und Lykaonien* (Denkschriften der Österreichischen Akademie der Wissenschaften, phil.-hist. Kl. 172) (Vienna)

Belke, K. 1996. *Tabula Imperii Byzantini 9: Paphlagonien und Honorias* (Denkschriften der Österreichischen Akademie der Wissenschaften, phil.-hist. Kl. 249) (Vienna)

Biggeli, A. 2015. 'Collections of edifying stories', in Efthymiadis 2014a: 143–160

Bikoulis, P., H. Elton, J.F. Haldon and J. Newhard. 2015. 'Above as below: application of multiple survey techniques at a Byzantine Church at Avkat', in K. Winther-Jacobsen and L. Summerer, *Landscape and settlement dynamics in Northern Anatolia in the Roman and Byzantine period* (Stuttgart): 101–117

Bourbou, Chr. and S.J. Garvie-Lock. 2009. 'Breastfeeding and weaning patterns in Byzantine times. Evidence from human remains and written sources', in Papaconstantinou and Talbot 2009: 65–83

Bowersock, G. 2002. *Martyrdom and Rome* (Cambridge)

Brandes, W. 1989. *Die Städte Kleinasiens im 7. und 8. Jahrhundert* (BBA 56) (Berlin)

Brooks, E.W. 1901. 'Arabic Lists of Byzantine Themes', *JHS* 21: 67–77

Broshi, M. 1974. 'The expansion of Jerusalem in the reigns of Hezekiah and Manasseh', *Israel Exploration Journal* 24: 21–26

Brown, P. 1981. *The cult of the saints. Its rise and function in Latin Christianity* (Chicago)

Browning, R. 1981. 'The 'low level' saint's life in the early Byzantine world', in S. Hackel, ed., *The Byzantine Saint* (London): 117–127

Brubaker, L. and J.F. Haldon. 2011. *Byzantium in the iconoclast era, c. 680–850. A history* (Cambridge)

Bryer, A.A.M. and D. Winfield. 1985. *The Byzantine monuments and topography of the Pontos*, 2 vols (Washington DC)

Cameron, Av. 1988. 'Eustratius's Life of the patriarch Eutychius and the fifth ecumenical council', in J. Chrysostomides, ed., *Kathegetria. Essays presented to Joan Hussey for her 80th birthday* (Camberley): 225–247

Cameron, Av. 1990. 'The Life of the patriarch Eutychius: models of the past in the late sixth century', in G. Clarke, ed., *Reading the past in late Antiquity* (Rushcutters Bay): 205–223

Campagnolo, M. and K. Weber. 2015. *Poids romano-byzantins et byzantions en alliage cuivreux.* Collections du Musée d'art et d'histoire – Genève (Milan)

Carrié, J.-M. and A. Rousselle. 1999. *L'Empire Romain en mutation: des Sévères à Constantin, 192–337* (Paris)

Caseau, B. Chevallier. 2009. 'Childhood in Byzantine saints' lives', in Papaconstantinou and Talbot 2009: 127–166

Castelli, E. 2004. *Martyrdom and memory: early Christian culture making* (New York–Chichester)

Cheynet, J.-Cl. 2003. 'Le culte de saint Théodore chez les officiers de l'armée d'Orient', in A. Avramea, A. Laiou and E. Chrysos, eds, *Byzantium. State and Society. In memory of Nikos Oikonomidès* (Athens): 137–154; repr. in J.-Cl. Cheynet, *La société byzantine. L'apport des sceaux*, 2 vols (Paris, 2008), I: 307–321

Cheynet, J.-Cl. 2006a. *The Byzantine aristocracy and its military function.* Aldershot

Cheynet, J.-Cl. 2006b. 'The Byzantine aristocracy (8th–13th centuries)', in Cheynet 2006a: I, 1–43

Conant, J. 2012. *Staying Roman. Conquest and identity in Africa and the Mediterranean, 439–700* (Cambridge)

Constas, N. 2002. 'An apology for the cult of saints in Late Antiquity: Eustratius Presbyter of Constantinople, On the state of souls after death (CPG 7522)', *Journal of Early Christian Studies* 10.2: 267–285

Coote, R.B. 1992. 'Siloam inscription', in D.N. Freedman et al., eds, *The Anchor Bible dictionary* (New York–London): 6, 23–24

Craft, S. forthcoming. 'Travel and communications', in J.F. Haldon, H. Elton and J. Newhard, eds, *Euchaïta: A Late Roman and Byzantine City in Anatolia. The Avkat archaeological survey* (Cambridge)

Crowfoot, J.W. 1929. 'The church of St. Theodore at Jerash', *Palestine Exploration Fund Quarterly Statement* 60: 17–36

Cumont, F. and E. Cumont. 1906. *Studia Pontica* (Brussels)

Dagron, G. 1984. 'Le culte des images dans le monde byzantin', in G. Dagron, *La romanité chrétienne en Orient* (London): 133–160

Dagron, G. 1992. 'L'ombre d'un doute: l'hagiographie en question, VIe–XIe siècle', *DOP* 46: 59–68

Dagron, G. and H. Mihaescu. 1986. *Le traité sur la Guérilla (De velitatione) de l'empereur Nicéphore Phocas (963–969).* Texte établi par Gilbert Dagron et Haralambie Mihaescu, trad. et comm. par G. Dagron (Paris)

Dal Santo, M. 2011. 'The God-protected empire? Scepticism towards the cult of saints in early Byzantium', in P. Sarris, M. Dal Santo and P. Booth, eds, *An age of saints? Power, conflict and dissent in early medieval Christianity* (Brill): 129–149

Daniélou, J. 1955. 'La chronologie des sermons de saint Grégoire de Nysse', *Revue des sciences religieuses* 29: 346–372

Danoff, C.M. 1962. 'Euxeinos Pontos', *RE Suppl.* ix: 866–1175

Darrouzès, J. 1989. 'Remarques sur les créations d'évêchés byzantins', *REB* 47: 209–237

De Jerphanion, G. 1914. *Carte du Bassin Moyen du Yechil Irmak, 1:200,000* (Paris)

De Ste Croix, G.E.M. 1963. 'Why were the early Christians persecuted?', *Past and Present* 26: 6–38

Delehaye, H. 1897. 'Les ménologes grecs', *AB* 16: 311–329

Delehaye, H. 1911. Review of Anderson et al. 1910, in *AB* 30: 366

Delehaye, H. 1921. *Les passions des martyrs et les genres littéraires* (Subsid. Hagiographica 13b) (Brussels, repr. Brussels 1966)

Delehaye, H. 1925a. See under Sources, above

Delehaye, H. 1925b. 'Les recueils antiques des miracles des saints', *AB* 43: 1–85, 305–325

Delehaye, H. 1933. *Les origines du culte des martyrs* (Subsidia hagiographica 20) (Brussels, repr. 2004)

Delehaye, H. 1966. 'Euchaïta et la légende de Saint Théodore', in H. Delehaye, *Mélanges d'hagiographie grecque et latine* (Brussels): 275–280 (orig. publ. as 'Euchaïta et la légende de S. Théodore', in W.H. Buckler and W.M. Calder, eds, *Anatolian Studies Presented to Sir William Mitchell Ramsay* [Manchester, 1923]: 129–134)

Der Nersessian, S. 1965. *Aght'amar: Church of the Holy Cross* (Cambridge)

Déroche, V. 1993. 'Pourqoi écrivait-on des recueils de miracles? L'exemple des miracles de Saint Artémios', in *Les saints et leur sanctuaires: textes, images et monuments* (Byzantina Sorbonensia 13) (Paris): 95–116

Detoraki, M. 2014. 'Greek passions of the martyrs in Byzantium', in Efthymiadis 2014a: 61–102

Deubner, L. 1907. *Kosmas und Damian* (Berlin–Leipzig)

Di Berardino, A. 2006. *Patrology. The eastern Fathers from the council of Chalcedon (451) to John of Damascus (+ 750)*, trans. A. Walford (Institutum Patristicum Augustinianum) (Cambridge)

Doublet, G. 1889. 'Inscriptions de Paphlagonie.' *BCH* 13: 293–319

Duffy, J. and E. Bourbouhakis. 2003. 'Five Miracles of St Menas', in J.W. Nesbitt, ed., *Byzantine authors: literary activities and preoccupations. Texts and translations dedicated to the memory of Nicholas Oikonomides* (Leiden/ Boston): 65–81

Efthymiadis, S. 1998. 'Hagiographica varia (9th–20th c.', *JöB* 48: 41–48 (repr. in S. Efthymiadis, *Hagiography in Byzantium. Literature, social history and cult* [Farnham, 2011]: IX)

Efthymiadis, S. 1999. 'Greek Byzantine collections of miracles: a chronological and bibliographical survey', *Symbolae Osloenses* 74: 195–211

Efthymiadis, S. 2011a. ed. *The Ashgate research companion to Byzantine hagiography, 1: periods and places* (Farnham)

Efthymiadis, S. 2011b. 'Hagiography from the "Dark age" to the age of Symeon Metaphrastes (eighth–tenth century)', in Efthymiadis 2011a: 95–142

Efthymiadis, S. 2011c. 'Versi su San Teodoro a proposito del miracolo dei "colivi" (*BHG* 1769): l'agiografia metrica al servizio della polemica antilatina', *Rivista di Studi Bizantini e Neoellenici* n.s. 48: 123–136

Efthymiadis, S. 2014a. ed. *The Ashgate research companion to Byzantine hagiography, 2: Genres and contexts* (Farnham)

Efthymiadis, S. 2014b. 'Collections of miracles (fifth–fifteenth centuries)', in Efthymiadis 2014a: 103–142

Efthymiadis, S. and N. Kalogeras. 2014. 'Audience, language and patronage in Byzantine hagiography', in Efthymiadis 2014a: 247–284

Efthymiadis, S., V. Déroche, A. Biggeli and Z. Aïnalis. 2011. 'Greek hagiography in late Antiquity (fourth–seventh centuries)', in Efthymiadis 2011a: 35–94

Elton, H. 1996. *Warfare in Roman Europe AD 350–425* (Oxford)

Erdkamp, P. 1998. *Hunger and the sword. Warfare and food supply in Roman republican wars (264 – 30 B.C.)* (Amsterdam)

Facella, M. and M. Stanke. 2011. 'Eine Inschriftenplatte für Theodoros Stratelates und weitere christliche Zeugnisse vom Dülük Baba Tepesi', in E. Winter, ed., *Von Kummuh nach Telouch. Archäologische und historische Untersuchungen in Kommagene* (Dolichener und Kommagenische Forschungen 4, AMS 64. Bonn): 157–186

Flusin, B. 2011. 'Palestinian hagiography (fourth–eighth centuries)', in Efthymiadis 2011a: 199–226

Follieri, E. 1962. 'Saba Goto e Saba Stratelata', *AB* 80: 249–307

Foss, C. and D. Winfield. 1986. *Byzantine fortifications* (Pretoria)

Foss, F. 2002. 'Pilgrimage in medieval Asia Minor', *DOP* 56: 129–151

Franchi de Cavalieri, P. 1909/1912. 'Attorno al più antico testo del martyrium S. Theodori Tironis', *Note agiografiche* 3 (Studi e testi 22. Rome): 91–107; *Note agiografiche* 4 (Studi e testi 24) (Rome, 1912): 161–185

Frankfurter, D. 2009. 'Martyrology and the prurient gaze', *Journal of Early Christian Studies* 17/2: 215–245

French, D. 1992. 'Amasian notes 2', *Epigraphica Anatolica* 20: 63–68

French, D. 1996. 'Amasian notes 3: Dated inscriptions from Amasia and its territory', *EA* 26: 70–86

Greenfield, R.P.H. 2000. see *Vita Lazari Gales*.

Grégoire, H. 1909. 'Rapport sur un voyage d'exploration dans dans le Pont et en Cappadoce', *BCH* 33: 3–169

Grégoire, H. 1910. 'Géographie byzantine', *BZ* 19: 59–62

Grégoire, H. 1922. *Recueils des inscriptions grecques chrétiennes d'Asie Mineure* (Paris)

Grig, L. 2004. *Making martyrs in Late Antiquity* (London)

Gross, A. 2005. *Spirituality and law: courting martyrdom in Christianity and Judaism* (Lanham, MD)

Grosse, R. 1915. 'Die Rangordnung der römischen Armee des 4.-6. Jahrhunderts', *Klio* (1915): 122–161

Grosse, R. 1920. *Römische Militärgeschichte von Gallienus bis zum Beginn der byzantinischen Themenverfassung* (Berlin)

Grotowski, P.Ł. 2010. *Arms and armour of the warrior saints. Tradition and innovation in Byzantine iconography (843–1261)* (Leiden)

Hahn, C. 1990. 'Loca sancta souvenirs: sealing the pilgrim's experience', in R. Ousterhout, ed., *The Blessings of Pilgrimage* (Urbana–Chicago): 85–96

Haldon, J.F. 1993. 'Military Service, Military Lands and the Status of Soldiers: Current Problems and Interpretations', *Dumbarton Oaks Papers* 47: 1–67

Haldon, J.F. 1997a. *Byzantium in the seventh century. The transformation of a culture* (2nd edn) (Cambridge)

Haldon, J.F. 1997b. 'The Miracles of Artemius and Contemporary Attitudes: Context and Significance', in J. Nesbitt and V. Crysafulli, eds, *The Miracles of Saint Artemius: Translation, Commentary and Analysis* (Washington DC): 33–73

Haldon, J.F. 1999. *Warfare, State and Society in the Byzantine World 550–1204* (London)

Haldon, J.F. 2007. '"Tortured by my conscience". The *Laudatio Therapontis*. A neglected source of the later seventh or early eighth century', in H. Amirav and B. ter Haar Romeney, eds, *From Rome to Constantinople. Studies in honour of Averil Cameron* (Leiden): 262–278

Haldon, J.F. 2009. 'Social élites, wealth and power', in J.F. Haldon, ed., *The social history of Byzantium* (Oxford): 168–211

Haldon, J.F. 2014. *A critical commentary on the Taktika of Leo V* (Dumbarton Oaks Studies 44) (Washington DC)

Haldon, J.F. and H. Kennedy. 1980. 'The Byzantine–Arab frontier in the eighth and ninth centuries: military organisation and society in the borderlands', *Zbornik Radova Vizantološkog Instituta* 19: 79–116

Haldon, J.F. and H. Elton, 2007. *The Euchaïta/Avkat Project. Preliminary short report on the Avkat Survey Project. Summer season, August–September 2007.* www.princeton.edu/avkat/reports

Haldon, J.F., H. Elton and J. Newhard. 2009. *The Avkat archaeological survey 2009.* www.princeton.edu/avkat/reports

Haldon, J.F., H. Elton and J. Newhard. 2010. *The Avkat archaeological survey 2010.* www.princeton.edu/avkat/reports

Haldon, J.F., H. Elton and J. Newhard. forthcoming. eds. *Euchaïta: A Late Roman and Byzantine City in Anatolia. The Avkat archaeological survey* (Cambridge)

Halkin, F. 1963. 'Inédits byzantins d'Ochrida, Candie et Moscou', *Subsidia* 38: 69–85

Halkin, F. 1974. *Martyrs grecs IIe–VIIIe s.* (London)

Halkin, F. 1981. 'L'éloge de Saint Théodore le Stratélate par Euthyme Protoasecretis', *AB* 99: 221–237

Hellenkemper, H. 1995. 'Frühe christliche Wallfahrtsstätten in Kleinasien', in E. Dassmann and J. Engemann, eds, *Akten des XII. Internationalen Kongresses für Christliche Archäologie, Bonn, 22.–28. September, 1991* (*Jahrbuch für Antike und Christentum*. Ergänzungsband 20; *Studi di antichità cristiana* 52) (Münster): 259–271

Hendy, M.F. 1985. *Studies in the Byzantine monetary economy, c.300–1450* (Cambridge)

Hengstenberg, W. 1912/1913. 'Der Drachenkampf des Heiligen Theodor', *Oriens Christianus* 2: 78–106; 3: 241–80; with 'Nachtrag zu dem Aufsatz "Der Drachenkampf des Heiligen Theodor"', *Oriens Christianus* 3: 135–137

Hinterberger, M. 2014a. 'Byzantine hagiography and its literary genres. Some critical observations', in Efthymiadis 2014a: 25–60

Hinterberger, M. 2014b. 'The Byzantine hagiographer and his text', in Efthymiadis 2014a: 211–246.

Hoepfner, W. 1966. *Herakleia Pontike* (Vienna)

Høgel, Chr. 2014. 'Symeon Metaphrastes and the metaphrastic movement', in Efthymiadis 2014a: 181–196

Holum, K. 1982. *Theodosian empresses: women and imperial dominion in late antiquity* (Berkeley, CA)

Honigmann, E. 1935. *Die Ostgrenze des byzantinischen Reiches von 363 bis 1071* (Brussels)

Howard-Johnston, J.D. 1995. 'The siege of Constantinople in 626', in C. Mango and G. Dagron, eds, *Constantinople and its hinterland* (Aldershot): 131–142

Hoyland, R.G. 1997. *Seeing Islam as others saw it. A survey and evaluation of Christian, Jewish and Zoroastrian writings on early Islam* (Studies in Late Antiquity and Early Islam 13) (Princeton, NJ)

Hutter, I. 1988. 'Theodorupolis', in I. Ševčenko and I. Hutter, eds, *AETOΣ. Studies in honour of Cyril Mango* (Stuttgart–Leipzig): 181–190

Janin, R. 1935. 'Les églises des saints militaires', *EO* 34: 56–70

Janin, R. 1937. 'Études de topographie byzantine: Emboloi tou Domninou. Tou Maurianou', *EO* 36: 137–49

Janin, R. 1964. *Constantinople byzantine. Développement urbain et repertoire topographique* (Paris)

Janin, R. 1969. *La géographie ecclésiastique de l'empire byzantin* 1.3: *Le siège de Constantinople et le patriarcat oecuménique: les églises et les monastères* (Paris)

Jankowiak, M. 2013. 'The *Notitia* 1 and the impact of Arab invasions on Asia Minor', *Millennium* 10: 435–461

Jeffreys, E.M. 2014. 'The afterlife of *Digenes Akrites*', in P. Roilos, ed., *Medieval Greek storytelling: fictionality and narrative in Byzantium* (Wiesbaden): 141–162

Jones, A.H.M. 1954. 'The date and value of the Verona list', *JRS* 44: 21–29

Jones, A.H.M. 1964. *The later Roman empire 284–602: a social and administrative survey* (Oxford)

Jones, A.H.M. 1971. *The cities of the eastern Roman provinces* (Oxford)

Kaegi, W.E. 2008. 'Confronting Islam: emperors versus Caliphs (641–c. 850)', in J. Shepard, ed., *Cambridge History of the Byzantine empire ca. 500–1492* (Cambridge): 365–394

Kaldellis, N. 2014. 'The hagiography of doubt and scepticism', in Efthymiadis 2014a: 453–477

Kalogeras, N. 2000. *Byzantine childhood education and its social role from the sixth century until the end of iconoclasm* (Ann Arbor, MI)

Kaplony, A. 1996. *Konstantinopel und Damaskos. Gesandtschaften und Verträge zwischen Kaisern und Kalifen 639–750. Untersuchungen zum Gewohnheits-Völkerrecht und zur interkulturellen Diplomatie* (Islamkundliche Untersuchungen 208) (Berlin)

Karpozilos, A. 1982. *Συμβολή στη Μελέτη τοῦ ἔργου τοῦ Ἰωάννη Μαυρόποδος* (Ioannina)

Kaster, R. 1983. 'Notes on "primary" and "secondary" education in Late Antiquity', *Transactions of the American Philological Association* 113: 323–346

Kazhdan, A. 1983. 'Hagiographical notes (1–4)', *B* 53: 544–545

Kazhdan, A. 1988. 'Hagiographical notes (17–20)', *Erytheia* 9.2: 197–200.

Kazhdan, A. 1993. 'Saint Andrew the Stratelates and Andrew the Stratelates, the Scythian', in J.S. Langdon, St W. Reinert, J.S. Allen and C.P. Ioannides, eds, Τὸ Ἑλληνικόν. *Studies in Honor of Speros Vryonis jr.* (New York): I, 145–152

Knauf, E.A. 1992. 'Ishmaelites', in D.N. Freedman et al., eds, *The Anchor Bible dictionary* (New York–London): 3, 315–320

Kominko, M. 2013. *The world of Kosmas. Illustrated Byzantine codices of the Christian Topography* (Cambridge)

Kosiński, R. 2010. *The Emperor Zeno: religion and politics* (Byzantina et slavica cracoviensia 6) (Cracow)

Lane, E. 1976. *Corpus monumentorum religionis dei Menis* III. *Interpretations and testimonia* (Leiden)

Lascaratos, J. and E. Poulakou-Rebelakou. 2003. 'Oribasius (fourth century) and early Byzantine perinatal nutrition', *Journal of Pediatric Gastroenterology and Nutrition* 36: 186–189

Leemans, J. 2006. "'At that time the group around Maximian was enjoying imperial power": an interpolation in Gregory of Nyssa's homily in praise of Theodore', *JThS* 57: 158–163

Lemerle, P. 1981. *Les plus anciens recueils des miracles de saint Démétrius et la pénétration des Slaves dans les Balkans*, 2: *Commentaire* (Paris)

Lenski, N. 2004. 'Empresses in the Holy Land. The creation of a Christian utopia in late antique Palestine', in L. Ellis and F.L. Kidner, eds, *Travel, communication and geography in Late Antiquity. Sacred and profane* (Aldershot): 114–124

LiDonnici, Lynn R. 1992. 'The images of Artemis Ephesia and Greco-Roman worship: a reconsideration', *Harvard Theological Review* 85: 389–415

Lilie, R.-J. 1976. *Die byzantinische Reaktion auf die Ausbreitung der Araber* (Misc. Byz. Monacensia 22) (Munich)

Limberis, V.M. 2011. *Architects of piety: the Cappadocian Fathers and the cult of the martyrs* (New York–Oxford)

Maas, P. 1912. 'Kontakion auf den hl. Theodoros unter dem Namen Romanos', *Oriens Christianus* 2: 48–69

Macrides, R. 1984. 'Justice under Manuel I Komnenos: four novels on court business and murder', *Fontes Minores* 6 (Frankfurt): 99–204 (repr. in R.J. Macrides, *Kinship and justice in Byzantium, 11th–15th centuries* [Aldershot, 1999]: IX)

Magdalino, P. 1989. 'Honour among Romaioi: the framework of social values in the world of Digenes Akrites and Kekaumenos', *BMGS* 13: 183–218

Mango, C. 1972. *The Art of the Byzantine Empire. Sources and Documents* (Englewood Cliffs, N.J.)

Mango, C. 1983. 'The Two Lives of St Ioannikios and the Bulgarians', in *Okeanos. Essays Presented to Ihor Ševčenko on his Sixtieth Birthday by his Colleagues and Students* (= *Harvard Ukrainian Studies* 7) (Cambridge, MA): 393–404

Mango, C. 1986a. 'The development of Constantinople as an urban centre', in *The 17th International Byzantine Congress, Major Papers* (Washington DC): 118–136

Mango, C. 1986b. 'Epigrammes honorifiques, statues et portraits à Byzance', in Ἀφιέρωμα στὸν Νίκο Σβορῶνο I (Rethymnon): 23–35

Mango, C. 1972. *The Art of the Byzantine Empire. Sources and Documents* (Englewood Cliffs, N.J.)

Mango, C. and I. Ševčenko. 1972. 'Three Inscriptions of the Reign of Anastasius I and Constantine V', *BZ* 65: 379–393

Maraval, P. 1985. *Lieux saints et pèlerinage* (Paris)

Mare, W. Harold. 1992a. 'Zion', in D.N. Freedman et al., eds, *The Anchor Bible dictionary* (New York–London): 6, 1096–1097

Mare, W. Harold. 1992b. 'Siloam, Pool of', in D.N. Freedman et al., eds, *The Anchor Bible dictionary* (New York–London): 6, 24–26

Markopoulos, A. 1986. 'Épistolaire du "Professeur Anonyme" de Londres', in Ἀφιέρωμα στὸν Νίκο Σβορῶνο I (Rethymnon): 139–144

Meyer, P. 1894. *Die Haupturkunden für die Geschichte der Athosklöster* (Leipzig)

Mitchell, S. 1993. *Anatolia: Land, men and gods in Asia Minor*, 2 vols (Oxford)

Moffatt, A. 1986. 'The Byzantine child', *Social Research* 53: 705–723

Moralee, J. 2006. 'The stones of St Theodore: disfiguring the pagan past in Christian Gerasa', *Journal of Early Christian Studies* 14: 183–215

Moss, C. 2013. *The myth of persecution: how early Christians invented a story of martyrdom* (New York)

Niewöhner, Ph., G. Dikilitaş, E. Erkul, S. Giese, J. Gorecki, W. Prochaska, D. Sarı, H. Stümpel, A. Vardar, A. Waldner, A. Walser and H. Woith. 2013. 'Bronze Age höyüks, Iron Age hilltop forts, Roman poleis and Byzantine pilgrimage in Germia and its vicinity. "Connectivity" and a lack of "definite places" on the central Anatolian high plateau', *Anatolian Studies* 63: 97–136

Oikonomidès, N. 1972. *Les listes de préséance byzantins des IXe–Xe siècles* (Paris)

Oikonomidès, N., 1986. 'Le dédoublement de S. Théodore et les villes d'Euchaïta et d'Euchaneia', *AB* 104: 327–335

Ohme, H. 1990. *Das Concilium Quinisextum und seine Bischofsliste. Studien zum Konstantinopler Konzil von 692* (Arbeiten zur Kirchengeschichte 56) (Berlin– New York)

Pancaroğlu, O. 2004. 'The itinerant dragon-slayer: forging paths of image and identity in medieval Anatolia', *Gesta* 43.2: 151–164

Papaconstantinou, A. and A.-M. Talbot. 2009. eds. *Becoming Byzantine. Children and childhood in Byzantium* (Cambridge, MA)

Paschalides, S.A. 1999. Νικήτας Δαβὶδ Παφλαγών τὸ πρόσωπο καὶ τὸ ἔργο του: Συμβολὴ στὴ μελέτη τῆς προσωπογραφίας καὶ τῆς ἁγιολογικῆς γραμματείας τῆς προμεταφραστικῆς περιόδου (Thessaloniki)

Patlagean, E. 1981. 'Sainteté et pouvoir', in S. Hackel, ed., *The Byzantine saint* (Birmingham) (= *Studies supplementary to Sobornost* 5): 88–105

Peeters, P. 1920. Review of P. Karolides, 'Bemerkungen zu den alten kleinasiatischen Sprachen und Mythen', *AB* 38: 191–195

Petit, L. 1898–1899. 'La grande controverse des colybes', *EO* 2: 321–331

Pitarakis, B. 2009. 'The material culture of childhood in Byzantium', in Papaconstantinou and Talbot 2009: 167–251

Pratsch, T. 2005. *Der hagiographische Topos. Griechische Heiligenviten in mittelbyzantinischer Zeit* (Berlin)

Prinzing, G. 2009. 'Observations on the legal status of children and the stages of childhood in Byzantium', in Papaconstantinou and Talbot 2009: 15–34

Quasten, J. 1950. *Patrology*, I: *The beginnings of Christian literature* (Utrecht 1950, repr. Westminster, MD, 1986)

Ramsay, W.M. 1890. *The Historical Geography of Asia Minor* (London; repr. Amsterdam, 1962).

Rapp, C. 1998. 'Storytelling as spiritual communication in early Greek hagiography', *Journal of Early Christian Studies* 6: 431–448

Rapp, C. 2005. *Holy bishops in Late Antiquity. The nature of Christian leadership in an age of transition* (Berkeley–Los Angeles–London)

Rhalles, K. and M. Potles. 1852–1859. Σύνταγμα τῶν θείων καὶ ἱερῶν κανόνων, 6 vols (Athens)

Riedel, M. 2010. 'Fighting the good fight: the Taktika of Leo VI and its influence on Byzantine cultural identity' (Oxford DPhil thesis)

Rochow, I. 1994. *Kaiser Konstantin V. (741–775). Materialien zu seinem Leben und Nachleben* (BBS 1) (Frankfurt a. M.)

Ronchey, S. 1990. *Indagine sul Martirio di San Policarpo: critica storica e fortuna agiografica di un caso giudiziario in Asia Minore* (Rome)

Rösch, G. 1978. Ὄνομα βασιλείας. *Studien zum offiziellen Gebrauch der Kaisertitel in spätantiker und frühbyzantinischer Zeit* (Byzantina Vindobonensia 10) (Vienna)

Ruge, W. 1936. 'Nikomedeia', in *RE* xvii.1: 468–492

Rydén, L. 1993. 'Gaza, Emesa and Constantinople: late ancient cities in the light of hagiography', in L. Rydén and J.O. Rosenqvist, eds, *Aspects of Late Antiquity and Early Byzantium* 4 (Stockholm): 133–144

Saradi, H. 1996. 'Notes on the *vita* of Saint Markianos', *Byzantinoslavica* 57: 18–25

Saradi, H. 2014. 'The city in Byzantine hagiography', in Efthymiadis 2014a: 419–452

Sasson, V. 1982. 'The Siloam tunnel inscription', *Palestine Exploration Quarterly* 14: 111–117

Schatkin, M.A., C. Blanc and B. Grillet. 2004. *Jean Chrysostome, Discours sur Babylas* (Sources Chrétiennes 362) (Paris)

Schneider, A.M. 1941. 'Brände in Konstantinopel', *BZ* 41: 382–403

Segal, J.B. 1970. *Edessa. The Blessed City* (Oxford)

Shahid, I. 1984a. *Rome and the Arabs* (Washington DC)

Shahid, I. 1984b. *Byzantium and the Arabs in the fourth century* (Washington DC)

Shahid, I. 1989. *Byzantium and the Arabs in the fifth century* (Washington DC)

Sinor, D. 1990. *The Cambridge History of early Inner Asia*, 1 (Cambridge)

Snee, R. 1998. 'Gregory Nazianzen's Anastasia church: Arianism, the Goths, and hagiography', *DOP* 52: 157–186

Starck, H. 1912. *Theodorus Teron. Textkritische Ausgabe der vormetaphrastischen Legende* (Freising)

Sullivan, D. 1998. 'The Life of Ioannikios', in A.-M. Talbot, ed., *Byzantine defenders of images: eight saints' lives in English translation* (Washington DC): 243–254

Talbert, R.J.A. 2000. *Barrington Atlas of the Greek and Roman world* (Princeton, NJ–Oxford)

Talbot, A.-M. 2008. 'Hagiography', in E. Jeffreys, J.F. Haldon and R. Cormack, eds, *The Oxford Handbook of Byzantine Studies* (Oxford): 862–871

Thierry, N. 1972. 'Art byzantin du haut Moyen-Age en Cappadoce. L'église no. 3 de Mavrucan', *Journal des savants* (1972): 233–269

Thierry, N. 1999. 'Aux limites du sacré et du magique. Un programme d'entrée d'une église en Cappadoce', *Res Orientales* 12: 233–247

Todt, K.-P. 1996. 'Theodor von Euchaita', in F.W. Bautz and T. Bautz, eds, *Biographisch-Bibliographisches Kirchenlexikon* (Hamm): 875–881

Trombley, F.R. 1985. 'The Decline of the Seventh-Century Town: The Exception of Euchaïta', in Sp. Vryonis, Jr., ed., *Byzantine Studies in Honor of Milton V. Anastos (Byzantina kai Metabyzantina* 4) (Malibu, CA): 65–90

Trombley, F.R. 1989. 'The Arab wintering raid against Euchaïta in 663/4', *Abstracts of the Fifteenth Annual Byzantine Studies Conference 1989* (Amherst, MA): 5–6

Trombley, F.R. 1993–1994. *Hellenic Religion and Christianization* (Religions in the Graeco-Roman World 115) (Leiden)

Vermaseren, M.J. 1977. *Cybele and Attis: the myth and the cult*, trans. A.M.H. Lemmers (London)

Vryonis, Sp. 1981. 'The Panēgyris of the Byzantine saint: a study in the nature of a medieval institution, its origins and fate', in S. Hackel, ed., *The Byzantine Saint* (London): 196–228

Walter, C. 1999. 'Theodore, archetype of the warrior saint', *REB* 57: 163–210

Walter, C. 2003a. 'Saint Theodore and the dragon', in C. Entwhistle, ed., *Through a glass brightly: studies in Byzantine and medieval art and archaeology presented to David Buckton* (Oxford): 95–106

Walter, C. 2003b. *The warrior saints in Byzantine art and tradition* (Aldershot)

Watters, M. and S. Wilkes. 2007. *Avkat archaeological project geophysical survey 2007*. www.princeton.edu/reports

Weigert, C. 1990. 'Theodor Stratelates (der Heerführer) von Euchaita', in W. Braunfels, ed., *Lexikon der christlichen Ikonographie* (Freiburg im Breisgau): 444–446

Weitzmann, K. 1976. *The monastery of Saint Catherine at Mount Sinai: the icons*, I, *From the sixth to the tenth century* (Princeton, NJ)

Whitby, M. and M. Whitby. 1989. *Chronicon paschale 284–628 AD. Translated with notes and introduction* (Liverpool)

White, M. 2008. 'The rise of the dragon in middle Byzantine hagiography', *BMGS* 32: 149–167

White, M. 2013. *Military saints in Byzantium and Rus, 900–1200* (Cambridge)

Winstedt, E.O. 1910. *Coptic Texts on St Theodore the General, on St Theodore the Eastern, on Chamoul and Justus* (London)

Witherington, B. 1984. *Women in the ministry of Jesus* (Cambridge)

Zandee, J. 1983. 'Vom heiligen Theodorus Anatolius. Ein doppelt überlieferter Text (koptisches Manuscript Utrecht 5)', *Vigiliae Christianae* 37: 288–305

Zuckerman, C. 1988. 'The Reign of Constantine V in the Miracles of St Theodore the Recruit (*BHG* 1764)', *REB* 46: 191–210

Zuckerman, C. 1991. 'Cappadocian Fathers and the Goths, B: Gregory of Nyssa's enkomion for St Theodore the recruit and the Gothic riots in Asia Minor in 379', *Travaux et Mémoires* 11: 479–86

INDEX

Printed and bound by CPI Group (UK) Ltd, Croydon, CR0 4YY

13/04/2025

14656566-0004